Getting Started with Impala

John Russell

To Kemal, Cheerio!)

Enjoy the ride!

John Russell

Beijing · Cambridge · Farnham · Köln · Sebastopol · Tokyo   O'REILLY®

Getting Started with Impala

by John Russell

Copyright © 2015 Cloudera, Inc. All rights reserved.

Printed in the United States of America.

Published by O'Reilly Media, Inc., 1005 Gravenstein Highway North, Sebastopol, CA 95472.

O'Reilly books may be purchased for educational, business, or sales promotional use. Online editions are also available for most titles (*http://safaribooksonline.com*). For more information, contact our corporate/institutional sales department: 800-998-9938 or *corporate@oreilly.com*.

Editor: Ann Spencer	**Cover Designer:** Ellie Volckhausen
Production Editor: Kristen Brown	**Interior Designer:** David Futato
Copyeditor: Gillian McGarvey	**Illustrator:** Rebecca Demarest
Proofreader: Linley Dolby	

October 2014:   First Edition

Revision History for the First Edition:

2014-09-19:   First release

See *http://oreilly.com/catalog/errata.csp?isbn=9781491905777* for release details.

ISBN: 978-1-491-90577-7

[LSI]

Table of Contents

Introduction

Cloudera Impala is an open source project that opens up the Apache Hadoop software stack to a wide audience of database analysts, users, and developers. The Impala massively parallel processing (MPP) engine makes SQL queries of Hadoop data simple enough to be accessible to analysts familiar with SQL and to users of business intelligence tools, and it's fast enough to be used for interactive exploration and experimentation.

From the ground up, the Impala software is written for high performance of SQL queries distributed across clusters of connected machines.

Who Is This Book For?

This book is intended for a broad audience of users from a variety of database, data warehousing, or Big Data backgrounds. It assumes that you're experienced enough with SQL not to need explanations for familiar statements such as **CREATE TABLE**, **SELECT**, **INSERT**, and their major clauses. Linux experience is a plus. Experience with the Apache Hadoop software stack is useful but not required.

This book points out instances where some aspect of Impala architecture or usage might be new to people who are experienced with databases but not the Apache Hadoop software stack.

The SQL examples in this book start from a simple base for easy comprehension, then build toward best practices that demonstrate high performance and scalability.

Conventions Used in This Book

The following typographical conventions are used in this book:

Italic
> Indicates new terms, URLs, email addresses, filenames, and file extensions.

Constant width

> Used for program listings, as well as within paragraphs to refer to program elements such as variable or function names, databases, data types, environment variables, statements, and keywords.

Constant width bold

> Shows commands or other text that should be typed literally by the user. This style is also used to emphasize the names of SQL statements within paragraphs.

Constant width italic

> Shows text that should be replaced with user-supplied values or by values determined by context.

 This element signifies a tip or suggestion.

 This element signifies a general note.

 This element indicates a warning or caution.

Using Code Examples

Supplemental material (code examples, exercises, etc.) is available for download at *https://github.com/oreillymedia/get-started-impala*.

This book is here to help you get your job done. In general, if example code is offered with this book, you may use it in your programs and documentation. You do not need to contact us for permission unless you're reproducing a significant portion of the code. For example, writing a program that uses several chunks of code from this book does not require permission. Selling or distributing a CD-ROM of examples from O'Reilly books does require permission. Answering a question by citing this book and quoting example code does not require permission. Incorporating a significant amount of example code from this book into your product's documentation does require permission.

We appreciate, but do not require, attribution. An attribution usually includes the title, author, publisher, and ISBN. For example: "*Getting Started with Impala* by John Russell (O'Reilly). Copyright 2015 Cloudera, Inc., 978-1-491-90577-7."

If you feel your use of code examples falls outside fair use or the permission given above, feel free to contact us at *permissions@oreilly.com*.

Safari® Books Online

 *Safari Books Online* is an on-demand digital library that delivers expert content in both book and video form from the world's leading authors in technology and business.

Technology professionals, software developers, web designers, and business and creative professionals use Safari Books Online as their primary resource for research, problem solving, learning, and certification training.

Safari Books Online offers a range of plans and pricing for enterprise, government, education, and individuals.

Members have access to thousands of books, training videos, and prepublication manuscripts in one fully searchable database from publishers like O'Reilly Media, Prentice Hall Professional, Addison-Wesley Professional, Microsoft Press, Sams, Que, Peachpit Press, Focal Press, Cisco Press, John Wiley & Sons, Syngress, Morgan Kaufmann, IBM Redbooks, Packt, Adobe Press, FT Press, Apress, Manning, New Riders, McGraw-Hill, Jones & Bartlett, Course Technology, and hundreds more. For more information about Safari Books Online, please visit us online.

How to Contact Us

Please address comments and questions concerning this book to the publisher:

O'Reilly Media, Inc.
1005 Gravenstein Highway North
Sebastopol, CA 95472
800-998-9938 (in the United States or Canada)
707-829-0515 (international or local)
707-829-0104 (fax)

We have a web page for this book, where we list errata, examples, and any additional information. You can access this page at *http://bit.ly/get-started-impala*.

To comment or ask technical questions about this book, send email to *bookquestions@oreilly.com*.

For more information about our books, courses, conferences, and news, see our website at *http://www.oreilly.com*.

Find us on Facebook: *http://facebook.com/oreilly*

Follow us on Twitter: *http://twitter.com/oreillymedia*

Watch us on YouTube: *http://www.youtube.com/oreillymedia*

Acknowledgments

I have to start by acknowledging the vision and execution of the Impala development team, led by Marcel Kornacker. I have learned a lot from them—especially Justin Erickson, Alex Behm, Lenni Kuff, Alan Choi, and Nong Li—that has made it into this book. Thanks to all the Impala team members and to Gwen Shapira, Mark Grover, Kate Ting, and Uri Laserson for their feedback and insights on my drafts.

Going a little further back, I've been lucky to be able to consult and collaborate with really good individuals and teams at each stage and transition in my career. Thanks to James Hamilton who convinced me to switch from programming languages to the database track all those years ago at IBM. Thanks to the late Mark Townsend at Oracle for many insights about the database industry. Thanks to Ken Jacobs who helped me switch into the open source group at Oracle, and the InnoDB team under Calvin Sun and later Sunny Bains for being great to work with and teaching me database internals. Thanks to Mike Olson and Justin Kestelyn at Cloudera for showing me the right way for a small company to tackle the enterprise software market, and to do developer and community outreach. Thanks to Paul Battaglia, Jolly Chen, and Frank Liva for building and supporting the Cloudera technical publications department.

Last but not least, this book would not be possible if not for my wonderful and supportive wife, Lotus Goldstein.

## CHAPTER 1

Why Impala?

The Apache Hadoop ecosystem is very data-centric, making it a natural fit for database developers with SQL experience. Much application development work for Hadoop consists of writing programs to copy, convert or reorganize, and analyze data files. A lot of effort goes into finding ways to do these things reliably, on a large scale, and in parallel across clusters of networked machines. Impala focuses on making these activities fast and easy, without requiring you to have a PhD in distributed computing, learn a lot of new APIs, or write a complete program when your intent can be conveyed with a single SQL statement.

Impala's Place in the Big Data Ecosystem

The Cloudera Impala project arrives in the Big Data world at just the right moment. Data volume is growing fast, outstripping what can be realistically stored or processed on a single server. The Hadoop software stack is opening that field up to a larger audience of users and developers.

Impala brings a high degree of flexibility to the familiar database ETL process. You can query data that you already have in various standard Hadoop file formats (see "File Formats" on page 21). You can access the same data with a combination of Impala and other Hadoop components such as Apache Hive, Apache Pig, and Cloudera Search without duplicating or converting the data. When query speed is critical, the Parquet columnar file format makes it simple to reorganize data for maximum performance of data warehouse-style queries.

Traditionally, Big Data processing has resembled batch jobs from the mainframe era where unexpected or tough questions required running jobs overnight or all weekend. The goal of Impala is to express even complicated queries directly with familiar SQL syntax, running fast enough that you can get an answer to an unexpected question in seconds or at most a few minutes. We refer to this human-scale type of responsiveness as "interactive."

For users and business intelligence tools that speak SQL, Impala brings a more effective development model than writing a new Java program to handle each new kind of analysis. Although the SQL language has a long history in the computer industry, with the combination of Big Data and Impala, it is once again cool.

Now you can write sophisticated analysis queries using natural expressive notation, the same way Perl mongers do with text-processing scripts. You can interactively traverse large data sets and data structures, like a Pythonista inside the Python shell. You can avoid memorizing verbose specialized APIs; SQL is like a RISC instruction set that focuses on a standard set of powerful commands. When you do need access to API libraries for capabilities such as visualization and graphing, you can access Impala data from programs written in languages such as C++, Java, and Python through the standard JDBC and ODBC protocols.

You can also take advantage of business tools that use SQL behind the scenes but don't require you to code SQL directly. For example, you can use traditional business intelligence tools such as IBM Cognos, SAP Business Objects, and MicroStrategy, as well as the new generation of data discovery tools such as Tableau.

Flexibility for Your Big Data Workflow

Impala integrates with existing Hadoop components, security, metadata, storage management, and file formats. You keep the flexibility you already have with these Hadoop strong points and add capabilities that make SQL queries much easier and faster than before.

With SQL, you can turn complicated analysis programs into simple, straightforward queries. To help answer questions and solve problems, you can enlist a wide audience of analysts who already know SQL or the standard business intelligence tools built on top of SQL. They know how to use SQL or BI tools to analyze large data sets and how to quickly get accurate answers for many kinds of business questions and "what if" scenarios. They know how to design data structures and abstractions that let you perform this kind of analysis both for common use cases and unique, unplanned scenarios.

The filtering, calculating, sorting, and formatting capabilities of SQL let you delegate those operations to the Impala query engine, rather than generating a large volume of raw results and coding client-side logic to organize the final results for presentation.

Impala embodies the Big Data philosophy that large data sets should be just as easy and economical to work with as small ones. Large volumes of data can be imported instantaneously, without any changes to the underlying data files. You have the flexibility to query data in its raw original form, or convert frequently queried data to a more compact, optimized form. Either way, you don't need to guess which data is worth saving; you preserve the original values, rather than condensing the data and keeping only the summarized form. There is no required step to reorganize the data and impose rigid structure, such as you might find in a traditional data warehouse environment.

The data files that Impala works with are all in open, documented, interoperable formats. (Some are even human-readable.) If you want to use Impala alongside other Hadoop components, you can do that without copying or converting the data. When you work with future generations of data-processing software, you can keep using the original data files rather than being faced with a difficult migration.

High-Performance Analytics

The Impala architecture provides such a speed boost to SQL queries on Hadoop data that it will change the way you work. Whether you currently use MapReduce jobs or even other SQL-on-Hadoop technologies such as Hive, the fast turnaround for Impala queries opens up whole new categories of problems that you can solve. Instead of treating Hadoop data analysis as a batch process that requires extensive planning and scheduling, you can get results any time you want them. Instead of doing a mental context switch as you wait for each query to finish, run a query, and immediately evaluate the results and fine-tune it. This rapid iteration helps you zero in on the best solution without disrupting your workflow. Instead of trying to shrink your data down to a representative subset, you can analyze everything you have, producing the most accurate answers and discovering new trends and correlations.

Perhaps you have had the experience of using software or a slow computer where after every command or operation, you waited so long that you had to take a coffee break or switch to another task. Then when you switched to faster software or upgraded to a faster computer, the system became so responsive that it lifted your mood, reengaged your intellect, and sparked creative new ideas. This is the type of reaction Impala aims to inspire in Hadoop users.

Exploratory Business Intelligence

Previously, if you were writing queries for business intelligence, the data typically had already been condensed to a manageable volume of high-value information, and gone through a complicated extract-transform-load (ETL) cycle to be loaded into a database system.

With Impala, this procedure is shortened. The data arrives in Hadoop after fewer steps, and Impala is ready to query it immediately. The high-capacity, high-speed storage of a Hadoop cluster lets you bring in all the data, not just the subset that you think is the most valuable. Because Impala can query the raw data files, you can skip the time-consuming stages of loading and reorganizing data that you might have encountered with older database systems.

This fast end-to-end process opens up new possibilities for analytic queries. You can use techniques such as exploratory data analysis (*http://en.wikipedia.org/wiki/Explora tory_data_analysis*) and data discovery (*http://en.wikipedia.org/wiki/Data_discovery*). With earlier generations of software, you were unlikely to do these kinds of operations: either because it was too expensive to store all the data in your data warehouse or too time-consuming to load and convert it all into a usable form.

You might receive raw data in simple formats such as delimited text files. Text files are bulky and not particularly efficient to query, but these aren't critical aspects for explor- atory business intelligence (BI). The queries you run against such data are intended to determine what new insights you can gather by analyzing a comprehensive set of data. You might spot trends, identify interesting subsets, and learn how to design a schema that matches well with the underlying structure of the data. Exploratory BI typically involves ad hoc queries: ones that are made up on the spot and then fine-tuned over several iterations. To tease out answers to questions such as "Are there any…?", "What is the most…?", and so on, the queries often involve aggregation functions such as MAX( ), MIN( ), COUNT( ), and AVG( ).

Once you know the queries you want to run on a regular basis, you can optimize your data and your schema to be as efficient as possible. For data you intend to intensively analyze, expect to graduate from text or other unoptimized file formats, and convert the data to a compressed columnar file format—namely the Parquet format. (If you are an experienced Hadoop shop, you might already be using Parquet format in your data pipeline. In that case, enjoy the extra query speed during the exploratory BI phase, and skip any subsequent data conversion steps.)

## CHAPTER 2

Getting Up and Running with Impala

Depending on your level of expertise with Apache Hadoop, and how much Hadoop infrastructure you already have, you can follow different paths to try out Impala.

 Some examples in this book use syntax, functions, and other features that were introduced in Impala 1.4, which is available both on Cloudera's CDH 5.1 and CDH 4 Hadoop distributions.

Installation

Cloudera Live Demo

The easiest way, with no installation required, is to use the Cloudera Live demo (*http://go.cloudera.com/cloudera-live.html*) (with optional sign-up). Using the Impala Query Editor through the Hue web interface, you can explore a few sample tables from the TPC-DS benchmark suite, enter SQL code to run queries, and even create your own tables and load data into them.

Cloudera QuickStart VM

If you are from a database background and a Hadoop novice, the Cloudera Quick-Start VM (*http://bit.ly/quickstart-VM*) lets you try out the basic Impala features straight out of the box. This single-node VM configuration is suitable to become familiar with the main Impala features. (For performance or scalability testing, you would graduate from this single-user, single-machine mode, and typically install the full CDH distribution using Cloudera Manager on a cluster of real machines or high-capacity VMs.) You run the QuickStart VM in VMWare, KVM, or VirtualBox, start the Impala service through the Cloudera Manager web interface, and then interact with Impala through the impala-shell interpreter or the ODBC and JDBC interfaces.

Cloudera Manager and CDH 5

For more serious testing or large-scale deployment, you can download and install the Cloudera Impala software as part of the CDH 5 distribution (*http://bit.ly/cdh5-dist*), and use it in a real cluster environment. You can freely install the software either through standalone packages or by using the Cloudera Manager *parcel* feature, which enables easier upgrades. You install the Impala server on each data node and designate one node (typically the same as the Hadoop namenode) to also run the Impala StateStore daemon. The simplest way to get up and running is through the Cloudera Manager application, where you can bootstrap the whole process of setting up a Hadoop cluster with Impala just by specifying a list of hostnames for the cluster.

Manual installation

Manual installation (*http://bit.ly/impala-manual*) is probably the least common method. Because this installation procedure must be applied to every data node in the cluster, it is most suitable for those familiar with managing distributed software, such as through Puppet or Chef.

Building from source

If you want to understand how Impala works at a deep level, you can get the Impala source code from GitHub (*https://github.com/cloudera/impala*) and build it yourself. Working with the C++ and Java source of Impala is a lot of fun, and you will learn a lot about distributed computing, but it is beyond the scope of this book, which is targeted towards SQL developers and business analysts.

No matter how you get started with Impala, you can join the open source project discussion through the newer discussion forum (*http://bit.ly/impala-discussion*) or the original mailing list (*http://bit.ly/google-impala-list*). See the full list of community resources (*http://impala.io/community.html*) on the dedicated Impala website.

Connecting to Impala

Whichever way you install Impala, at the end of the process you start some Impala-related daemons (`impalad`, `catalogd`, and `statestored`) on every data node in the cluster. The Cloudera Manager installation path bundles these daemons together as an *Impala service* that you can start and stop as a single unit.

The most convenient and flexible way to access Impala, and the one this book focuses on, is through the interactive `impala-shell` interpreter. In a development environment, before enabling all the industrial-grade security features, all you need to know is the hostname of any of the servers in the cluster where Impala is running. Impala's query engine is fully decentralized; you can connect to any data node, issue queries, and the work is automatically distributed across the cluster.

`impala-shell` defaults to connecting to `localhost`, which is convenient if you're running in a single-node VM, or you have a login on one of these data nodes in the cluster. To connect to a remote server, specify the `-i` option. If the port is different from the default of 21000, specify both host and port in the argument to the `-i` option.

The following examples show how you can connect to an Impala server running on the same machine where you are logged in:

```
$ ssh impala_coder@host07.dev_test_cluster.example.com
$ impala-shell
[localhost:21000] > show databases;
```

Or connect to an Impala server on a remote system:

```
$ ssh my_login@personal_linux_server.example.com
$ impala-shell -i host12.dev_test_cluster.example.com
[host12.dev_test_cluster.example.com:21000] > show tables;
```

Or connect to a remote system where Impala is listening on a nondefault port:

```
$ impala-shell -i host33.dev_test_cluster.example.com:27000
[host33.dev_test_cluster.example.com:27000] > create table foo (x int);
```

This initial phase, where you can connect from anywhere, is for early development experiments only. Until you set up security features such as SSL, authorization, and authentication, anyone else can connect to your Impala instance, possibly messing up your work or slowing down performance. Setting up security requires putting on your administrator hat or enlisting the assistance of your network administrator, and thus is beyond the scope of this book. Consult the Impala security documentation (*http://bit.ly/impala-security*).

Your First Impala Queries

To ease you through the learning phase, here are some queries you can try. In addition to demonstrating some of Impala's standard SQL syntax, these queries confirm whether your installation and configuration were successful.

To get your feet wet with the basic elements of Impala query syntax such as the underlying data types and expressions, you can run queries without any table or **WHERE** clause at all:

```
SELECT 1;
SELECT 2+2;
SELECT SUBSTR('Hello world',1,5);
SELECT CAST(99.5 AS INT);
SELECT CONCAT('aaa',"bbb",'ccc');
SELECT 2 > 1;
SELECT NOW() + INTERVAL 3 WEEKS;
```

Queries like this are useful for experimenting with arithmetic expressions, data type conversions, and built-in functions. You will see more examples of this technique in "Tutorial: Queries Without a Table" on page 49.

Because Impala does not have any built-in tables, running queries against real data requires a little more preparation. In the following example, we'll use the **INSERT ...** **VALUES** statement to create a couple of "toy" tables. (For scalability reasons, the VALUES clause is not really suitable when working with data of any significant volume, so expect to use **INSERT ... SELECT** instead in real production environments.)

```
-- Set up a table to look up names based on abbreviations.
CREATE TABLE canada_regions (name STRING, abbr STRING);

-- Set up a potentially large table
-- with data values we will use to answer questions.
CREATE TABLE canada_facts
  (id STRING, sq_mi INT, population INT);

-- The INSERT statement either appends to existing data in
-- a table via INSERT INTO, or replaces the data entirely
-- via INSERT OVERWRITE.

INSERT INTO canada_regions VALUES
  ("Newfoundland and Labrador" ,"NL"),
  ("Prince Edward Island","PE"),
  ("New Brunswick","NB"), ("Nova Scotia","NS"),
  ("Quebec","PQ"), ("Ontario","ON"),
  ("Manitoba","MB"), ("Saskatchewan","SK"), ("Alberta","AB"),
  ("British Columbia","BC"), ("Yukon","YT"),
  ("Northwest Territories","NT"), ("Nunavut","NU");

INSERT OVERWRITE canada_facts VALUES ("NL",156453,514536),
  ("PE",2190,140204), ("NB",28150,751171), ("NS",21345,921727),
  ("PQ",595391,8054756), ("ON",415598,13505900),
  ("MB",250950,1208268), ("SK",251700,1033381),
  ("AB",255541,3645257), ("BC",364764,4400057),
  ("YT",186272,33897), ("NT",519734,41462), ("NU",78715,31906);

-- We can query a single table, multiple tables via joins,
-- or build new queries on top of views.
SELECT name AS "Region Name" FROM canada_regions
  WHERE abbr LIKE 'N%';
+---------------------------+
| region name               |
+---------------------------+
| Newfoundland and Labrador |
| New Brunswick             |
| Nova Scotia               |
| Northwest Territories     |
| Nunavut                   |
+---------------------------+
```

```
-- This join query gets the population figure from one table
-- and the full name from another.
SELECT canada_regions.name, canada_facts.population
  FROM canada_facts JOIN canada_regions
  ON (canada_regions.abbr = canada_facts.id)
  ORDER BY population DESC;
```

```
+---------------------------+------------+
| name                      | population |
+---------------------------+------------+
| Ontario                   | 13505900   |
| Quebec                    | 8054756    |
| British Columbia          | 4400057    |
| Alberta                   | 3645257    |
| Manitoba                  | 1208268    |
| Saskatchewan              | 1033381    |
| Nova Scotia               | 921727     |
| New Brunswick             | 751171     |
| Newfoundland and Labrador | 514536     |
| Prince Edward Island      | 140204     |
| Northwest Territories     | 41462      |
| Yukon                     | 33897      |
| Nunavut                   | 31906      |
+---------------------------+------------+
```

```
-- A view is an alias for a longer query, and takes no time or
-- storage to set up.
-- Querying a view avoids repeating clauses over and over,
-- allowing you to build complex queries that are still readable.
CREATE VIEW atlantic_provinces AS SELECT * FROM canada_facts
  WHERE id IN ('NL','PE','NB','NS');
CREATE VIEW maritime_provinces AS SELECT * FROM canada_facts
  WHERE id IN ('PE','NB','NS');
CREATE VIEW prairie_provinces AS SELECT * FROM canada_facts
  WHERE id IN ('MB','SK','AB');
```

```
-- Selecting from a view lets us compose a series of
-- filters and functions.
SELECT SUM(population) AS "Total Population"
  FROM atlantic_provinces;
```

```
+------------------+
| total population |
+------------------+
| 2327638          |
+------------------+
```

```
SELECT AVG(sq_mi) AS "Area (Square Miles)"
  FROM prairie_provinces;
```

```
+---------------------+
| area (square miles) |
+---------------------+
| 252730.3333333333   |
+---------------------+
```

For more examples of tables and queries, starting from simple scenarios and working up to partitioned multigigabyte tables, see Chapter 5.

 As mentioned previously, **INSERT ... VALUES** is not a scalable way of bringing big volumes of data into Impala, and the data it produces is not organized for efficient querying. In fact, most of the large-scale data you work with will probably originate outside of Impala, then be brought in by **LOAD DATA** statements, and copied and transformed from table to table by **INSERT ... SELECT** statements operating on millions or billions of rows at a time. For examples of these techniques, see "Getting Data into an Impala Table" on page 27.

## CHAPTER 3

Impala for the Database Developer

As a database developer who knows SQL, you are in an ideal position to jump in and start using Impala right away.

This section covers some of the background information and coding techniques that help you start down the path to high performance and scalability, as you graduate from dedicated development and test environments to huge data sets on production clusters running under heavy load.

When you come to Impala from a background with a traditional relational database product, you find the same familiar SQL query language and DDL statements. Data warehouse experts will already be familiar with the notion of partitioning. If you have only dealt with smaller OLTP-style (online transaction processing) databases, the emphasis on large data volumes will expand your horizons.

 You might find that a certain SQL idiom is not yet supported in Impala, or your favorite built-in function from database system XYZ is not available yet. If so, don't be discouraged. You can often work around these with a simple query change. Because Impala is often used in organizations that already have substantial database infrastructure, prioritize which kinds of workloads you can try out with Impala in the short term. You might find that you can save many hours in your data pipeline or queries, even when only using Impala in a few places. Impala roadmap items (*http://bit.ly/impala-roadmap*) are regularly introduced, so check the New Features page (*http://bit.ly/impala-new*) often.

The SQL Language

The great thing about coming to Impala with relational database experience is that the query language is completely familiar: it's just SQL! (See the Impala SQL Language Reference (*http://bit.ly/impala-sql-lang-ref*) for all the supported statements and functions.) The **SELECT** syntax works like you're used to, with joins, views, relational operators, aggregate functions, ORDER BY and GROUP BY, casts, column aliases, built-in functions, and so on.

The original core column data types are STRING for all string and character data; INT and its cousins such as TINYINT and BIGINT for integers; FLOAT and DOUBLE for floating-point values; TIMESTAMP for all date- and time-related values; and BOOLEAN for true/false conditions. The Impala 1.4 release introduced DECIMAL for high-precision floating-point values (especially currency).

The **CREATE TABLE** and **INSERT** statements incorporate some of the format clauses that you might expect to be part of a separate data-loading utility, because Impala is all about the shortest path to ingest and analyze data.

The **EXPLAIN** statement provides a logical overview of statement execution. Instead of showing how a query uses indexes, the Impala **EXPLAIN** output illustrates how parts of the query are distributed among the nodes in a cluster, and how intermediate results are combined at the end to produce the final result set.

Standard SQL

Impala implements SQL-92 standard features for queries, with some enhancements from later SQL standards.

Limited DML

Because Hadoop Distributed File System (HDFS) is optimized for bulk insert and append operations, Impala currently doesn't have OLTP-style Data Manipulation Language (DML) operations such as **DELETE** or **UPDATE**. It also does not have indexes, constraints, or foreign keys; data warehousing experts traditionally minimize their reliance on these relational features because they involve performance overhead that can be too much when dealing with large amounts of data.

If you have new raw data files, you use **LOAD DATA** to move them into an Impala table directory. If you have data in one table that you want to copy into another table, optionally filtering, transforming, and converting in the process, you use an **INSERT ...** **SELECT** statement. If there is something not satisfactory about some set of data, you replace entire tables or partitions with an **INSERT OVERWRITE** statement.

No Transactions

The typical OLTP example of depositing to a bank account and withdrawing at the same time is not really appropriate for a data warehousing context. That's only one row! Impala is intended to analyze what happens across millions or billions of banking operations, ticket purchases, web page visits, and so on.

Impala only appends or replaces; it never actually updates existing data. In write operations, Impala deals not with one row at a time, but millions of rows through statements such as **LOAD DATA** and **INSERT ... SELECT**. Even on a transactional DBMS, this volume of new data can be impractical to roll back.

Rather than deleting arbitrary rows with a **DELETE** statement, you delete large groups of related rows at once, either through **DROP TABLE** or **ALTER TABLE ... DROP PARTITION**. If you make a mistake, the original files are still recoverable from the HDFS trashcan.

Operations performed directly in Impala work like the "autocommit" settings available on some database systems. All Impala nodes in the cluster are notified about new data from a **LOAD DATA** or **INSERT** statement, or DDL operations such as **CREATE TABLE** and **DROP TABLE**.

Remember that Impala has the flexibility to operate on data produced by external programs and pipelines too. When new files are deposited in an Impala table directory by some non-Impala command, the Impala **REFRESH** *table_name* statement acts much like a traditional **COMMIT** statement, causing Impala to re-evaluate the data in that table at the current moment.

Numbers

Early releases of Impala included binary-style numeric types: 8-bit, 16-bit, 32-bit, and 64-bit integer types, and 32-bit and 64-bit IEEE-754-style floating-point types. These types are well-suited to the kinds of scientific processing and numerical analysis done by many of the Impala early adopters. The following example shows queries with the basic integer and floating-point types.

```
-- STORE_ID is a SMALLINT, a 32-bit integer that holds up to 32,767.
SELECT DISTINCT(store_id) FROM sales_data;
-- DEGREES is a DOUBLE, a floating-point number from a sensor.
SELECT cos(degrees) FROM telemetry_data;
```

Impala 1.4 adds support for the DECIMAL data type, which represents base 10 values with varying numbers of significant digits. This type is well-suited for currency calculations, opening up Impala for a range of use cases with financial data. You can also use it to hold integer values with a larger range than the INT or even BIGINT types.

This example shows how with a DECIMAL value (in this case, three digits after the decimal point and nine digits total precision), you get back exactly the value you started with. For some fractional values, FLOAT and DOUBLE are very close but cannot represent them precisely. The extra predictability and accuracy during mathematical operations makes DECIMAL convenient for columns used with GROUP BY, comparisons to literal values, summing large numbers of values, and other cases where the inexact fractional representation of FLOAT and DOUBLE could cause problems.

```
CREATE TABLE dec_vs_float (dec DECIMAL(9,3), flt FLOAT, dbl DOUBLE);
INSERT INTO dec_vs_float VALUES (98.6,cast(98.6 AS FLOAT),98.6);
SELECT * FROM dec_vs_float;
+--------+------------------+------------------+
| dec    | flt              | dbl              |
+--------+------------------+------------------+
| 98.600 | 98.59999847412109 | 98.59999999999999 |
+--------+------------------+------------------+
```

In this example, the DEC column can represent the value 98.600 exactly, but we didn't define enough fractional digits to precisely represent 98.6001 or 98.5999. The 3 in the DECIMAL(9,3) declaration means the column only stores 3 digits after the decimal point. Therefore, with DECIMAL values, you decide in advance how many overall digits and fractional digits are required to represent all the relevant values.

Recent Additions

Impala's SQL functionality grows with each release. Here are some of the high points from the Impala 1.4 (July 2014) release. Because this book was finalized well in advance of the Impala 2.0 release, the first edition doesn't include examples of those new features. Always check the Impala new features documentation page (*http://bit.ly/impala-new-feat*) to see what SQL enhancements (along with other kinds of features) were added recently.

Early Impala releases required intermediate results for ORDER BY queries to fit in memory. In terms of syntax, all ORDER BY queries had to also include a LIMIT clause to cap the size of the result set. Impala 1.4 lifts this restriction, saving intermediate sort results to a disk scratch area when necessary.

The DECIMAL data type, introduced in Impala 1.4, lets Impala represent currency data with the kind of accuracy and rounding characteristics that are ideal for financial analysis. See "Numbers" on page 13 for more on the DECIMAL type.

Each release of Impala includes additional built-in functions, particularly for math and date/time operations. Impala 1.4 introduced EXTRACT() and TRUNC() for date/time values, and STDDEV() and VARIANCE() for statistical processing.

Big Data Considerations

The guidelines throughout this book typically apply to use cases that involve Big Data. But how big is Big, and what are the implications for your workflow, database schema, and SQL code?

Billions and Billions of Rows

Although Impala can work with data of any volume, its performance and scalability shine when the data is large enough that you can't produce, manipulate, and analyze it in reasonable time on a single server. Therefore, after you do your initial experiments to learn how all the pieces fit together, you very quickly scale up to working with tables containing billions of rows and gigabytes, terabytes, or even larger of total volume. The queries that you tinker with might involve data sets bigger than you ever used before.

You might have to rethink your benchmarking techniques if you're used to using smaller volumes, meaning millions of rows or a few tens of gigabytes. You'll start relying on the results of analytic queries because the scale will be bigger than you can grasp through your intuition. You'll become used to adding a LIMIT clause to many exploratory queries to prevent unexpected huge result sets.

Terminology Tip

In this book, when I refer to "a billion" of anything, I mean the US billion: one thousand million. 10^9. 100 Indian crore. When talking about gigabytes, I am referring to the disk or network gigabyte (a round number of one billion bytes) rather than the memory gigabytes (2^{30} bytes, also sometimes called a gibibyte).

The main exception to this rule is for Parquet files, where the data is buffered in memory up to one gibibyte and then that same amount is written to disk.

For problems that do not tax the capabilities of a single machine, many alternative techniques offer about the same performance. After all, if all you want to do is sort or search through a few files, you can do that plenty fast with Perl scripts or Unix commands such as grep. The Big Data issues come into play when the files are too large to fit on a single machine, when you want to run hundreds of such operations concurrently, or when an operation that takes only a few seconds for megabytes of data takes hours or even days when the data volume is scaled up to gigabytes or petabytes.

You can learn the basics of Impala SQL and confirm that all the prerequisite software is configured correctly using tiny data sets, as in most examples in Chapters 1-4. That's what we call a *canary test*, to make sure all the pieces of the system are hooked up properly.

To start exploring scenarios involving performance testing, scalability, and multinode cluster configurations, you typically use much, much larger data sets. Later on, in "Tutorial: The Journey of a Billion Rows" on page 51, we'll generate a billion rows of synthetic data. Then when the raw data is in Impala, we'll experiment with different combinations of file formats, compression codecs, and partitioning schemes. We'll even try some join queries involving a million billion combinations.

Don't put too much faith in performance results that involve only a few megabytes or gigabytes of data. Only when you blow past the data volume that a single server could reasonably handle, or saturate the I/O channels of your storage array, can you fully appreciate the performance increase of Impala over competing solutions and the effects of the various tuning techniques. To really be sure, do trials using volumes of data similar to your real-world system.

If today your data volume is not at this level, next year it might be. Don't wait until your storage is almost full (or even half full) to set up a big pool of HDFS storage on cheap commodity hardware. Whether or not your organization has already adopted the Apache Hadoop software stack, experimenting with Cloudera Impala is a valuable exercise to future-proof your enterprise.

HDFS Block Size

Because an HDFS data block contains up to 128 MB by default, you can think of any table less than 128 MB as small (tiny, even). That data could be represented in a single data block, which would be processed by a single core on a single server, with no parallel execution at all. In a partitioned table, the data for each partition is physically split up. Therefore, a table partition of less than 128 MB is in the same situation with limited opportunity for parallel execution. It's true that the 128 MB block might be split into several smaller files that are processed in parallel. Still, with such small amounts of data, it's hardly worth the overhead to send the work to different servers across the cluster.

Parquet Files: The Biggest Blocks of All

When it comes to Parquet files, Impala writes data files with a default block size of 1 GB. This design choice means that Impala is perfectly happy to process tables or even partitions with many, many gigabytes. For example, if you have a 100-node cluster with 16 cores per node, Impala could potentially process 1.6 TB of Parquet data in parallel, if nothing else were running on the cluster. Larger data volumes would only require a little waiting for the initial set of data blocks to be processed.

Because many organizations do not have those kinds of data volumes, you can decrease the block size before inserting data into a Parquet table. This technique creates a greater number of smaller files. You still want to avoid an overabundance of tiny files, but you might find a sweet spot at 256 MB, 128 MB, 64 MB, or even a little smaller for the Parquet block size. The key is to have enough data files to keep the nodes of the cluster busy, without those files being so small that the overhead of parallelizing the query swamps the performance benefit of parallel execution.

How Impala Is Like a Data Warehouse

With Impala, you can unlearn some notions from the RDBMS world. Long-time data warehousing users might already be in the right mindset, because some of the traditional database best practices naturally fall by the wayside as data volumes grow and raw query speed becomes the main consideration. With Impala, you will do less planning for normalization, skip the time and effort that goes into designing and creating indexes, and worry less about full-table scans.

Impala, as with many other parts of the Hadoop software stack, is optimized for fast bulk read and data load operations. Many data warehouse-style queries involve either reading all the data ("What is the highest number of different visitors our website ever had in one day?") or reading some large set of values organized by criteria such as time ("What were the total sales for the company in the fourth quarter of last year?"). Impala divides up the work of reading large data files across the nodes of a cluster. Impala also does away with the performance and disk space overhead of creating and maintaining indexes, instead taking advantage of the multimegabyte HDFS block size to read and process high volumes of data in parallel across multiple networked servers. As soon as you load the data, it's ready to be queried. Impala can run efficient ad hoc queries against any columns, not just preplanned queries using a small set of indexed columns.

In a traditional database, normalizing the data and setting up primary key/foreign key relationships can be time-consuming for large data volumes. That is why data warehouses (and also Impala) are more tolerant of denormalized data, with values that are duplicated and possibly stored in raw string form rather than condensed to numeric IDs. The Impala query engine works very well for data warehouse-style input data by doing bulk reads and distributing the work among nodes in a cluster. Impala can even automatically condense bulky, raw data into a data-warehouse-friendly layout as part of a conversion to the Parquet file format.

When executing a query involves sending requests to several servers in a cluster, Impala minimizes total resource consumption (disk I/O, network traffic, and so on) by making each server do as much local processing as possible before sending back the results. Impala queries typically work on data files in the multimegabyte or gigabyte range, whereas a server can read through large blocks of data very quickly. Impala does as much filtering and computation as possible on the server that reads the data, to reduce overall network traffic and resource usage on the other nodes in the cluster. Thus, Impala can very efficiently perform *full table scans* of large tables, the kinds of queries that are common in analytical workloads.

Impala makes use of partitioning, another familiar notion from the data warehouse world. Partitioning is one of the major optimization techniques you'll employ to reduce disk I/O and maximize the scalability of Impala queries. Partitioned tables physically divide the data based on one or more criteria, typically by date or geographic region, so that queries can filter out irrelevant data and skip the corresponding data files entirely. Although Impala can quite happily read and process huge volumes of data, your query will be that much faster and more scalable if a query for a single month only reads one-twelfth of the data for that year, or if a query for a single US state only reads one-fiftieth of the data for the entire country. Partitioning typically does not impose much overhead on the data loading phase; the partitioning scheme usually matches the way data files are already divided, such as when you load a group of new data files each day. In "Working with Partitioned Tables" on page 39, we'll see some examples of partitioned tables and queries.

Physical and Logical Data Layouts

When you're thinking in SQL, you're primarily concerned with the logical level. Your data is divided into tables, which have columns, and each column has a data type. Views let you impose a different logical arrangement without changing the actual tables and columns. Built-in functions and user-defined functions help to hide implementation details for complicated comparisons and computations.

Impala does not enforce constraints such as unique columns, NOT NULL constraints, or foreign keys. You validate those aspects earlier in the data pipeline.

The physical aspects come into play for performance. When you have a day's worth of data to ingest, can you finish all the necessary file operations before the next day's data is ready? That question depends on whether you need to copy, reorganize, or convert the data files. When you run queries, how much data is read from disk, how much memory is required, and how fast do the responses come back? The answer depends on physical aspects such as file format and partitioning.

The HDFS Storage Model

Data stored in Impala is stored in HDFS (*http://bit.ly/1s6P8kC*), a distributed filesystem mounted on one or more Linux servers. When a file is stored in HDFS, the underlying filesystem takes care of making it available across the cluster. Each data block within the file is automatically replicated to some number of hosts (typically at least three), so that all the data is still retrievable if one or two machines experience a hardware, software, or network problem. And when a block needs to be read and processed, that work can be farmed out to any of the servers that hold a copy of that block.

HDFS data blocks are much, much larger than you might have encountered on previous systems. The HDFS block size is typically in the tens of megabytes—often 128 MB or 64 MB. This size is more like what you see with data warehouse software or dedicated analytic hardware appliances. HDFS avoids the issue of wasteful writes by being an append-only filesystem. By reducing the number of possible operations, it focuses on doing a few things well: speed, reliability, and low cost.

Distributed Queries

Distributed queries are the heart and soul of Impala. Once upon a time, you needed a doctorate in parallel computing to even be able to think about doing such esoteric, obscure operations. Now, with Impala running on Hadoop, you just need…a laptop! And ideally, also an IT department with a cluster of Linux servers running Cloudera Distribution with Hadoop (CDH). But in a pinch, a single laptop with a VM will work for development and prototyping.

When an Impala query runs on a Hadoop cluster, Impala breaks down the work into multiple stages and automatically sends the appropriate requests to the nodes in the cluster. This automatic division of labor is why Impala is so well-suited to Big Data use cases. Queries that would strain the capacity of a single machine are a snap to run when the work can be divided between 4, 10, 100, or more machines. There is some overhead to dividing up the work and scheduling it across so many machines, which is why it is important to organize your schema for efficient query processing, and to help Impala estimate how much work is involved for a particular query.

The execution steps for each distributed query go something like this (greatly simplified):

1. Node #1, core #1: Read this portion of that gigantic data file. I know you have the relevant data block on your local storage device.

2. Node #1, core #2: Read a different portion of the same file. Each request like this goes to a node that has one of the replicated copies of the particular block. The multicore aspect means that each server can potentially process 4, 8, 16, or more data blocks in parallel.

3. Node #2, core #1: Read this entire small data file. It is small enough to fit in a single HDFS block, so you'll process the whole thing.

4. Repeat for all the data nodes in the cluster and cores on each node, up to the number of disks available for each node. Keep going until all relevant HDFS blocks have been processed.

5. Only columns X, Y, and Z are needed to process the query and produce the result set. Each node: Ignore the data from all other columns. (With Parquet format, this ignored data never gets read at all.) This operation is known as *projection*.

6. Each node: As you read the data file, ignore all the rows that don't match the WHERE clause. This is a *filtering* operation; the conditions in the WHERE clause are referred to as *predicates*.

7. Each node: Now take the more manageable amount of data that remains and do summing, sorting, grouping, function calls, or other manipulation on it.

8. Go through these steps for all the relevant data files in the table until all the needed data has been read and each core on each node has its own portion of the result set.

9. Condense the result set even more if the query has a LIMIT clause. Each node: Assume you are the one that found all the "top N" results, and send back a result set with only N rows.

10. Now if there is a JOIN or a UNION clause, each node transmits the intermediate results where necessary to other nodes that perform cross-checking, duplicate elimination, and so on. Repeat for all join and union clauses.

11. When all of the intermediate results are ready for all stages of the query, do as much consolidation as possible on the remote nodes, and then send final or almost-final results back to whichever node initiated the query in the first place. This *coordinator* node does any necessary final sorting, grouping, and aggregating. For example, the final determinations such as "top 10 visitors" can only be made when all the intermediate results can be compared against each other.

All of this parallel processing has implications for the nature of the results:

- Any write operations potentially produce multiple output files, with each node sending back its own contribution as a separate file.

- Which data is processed by which node is not fixed ahead of time. Thus, there's some degree of performance variation on consecutive queries.

- You cannot rely on the results on disk being returned in a particular order by subsequent queries. The work might be spread out differently among the nodes, or intermediate results might be returned in a different order depending on how fast each node finishes its part.

- The planning phase for each query tries to resolve as many unknowns as possible before distributing the work across the cluster. Impala turns expressions into constants wherever possible rather than re-evaluating them on each node. When you call a time-related function such as NOW(), that moment in time is captured at the start of the query, and the same value is used on all the nodes. It is not re-evaluated at the exact moment that each node starts working.

- The time needed to transmit final results back to the coordinator node is proportional to the size of the result set. Thus, Impala queries typically avoid SELECT * for wide tables, and typically include multiple WHERE clauses, a LIMIT clause, or aggregate functions to condense the results to a relatively small volume and minimize network overhead.

Normalized and Denormalized Data

One of the great debates in the database world is about normalization and denormalization.

Normalization means splitting columns into separate tables, and referring to the original column values through unique IDs, instead of repeating long strings such as a city name. This is a very popular technique in OLTP systems, where rarely updated data is separated out to speed up updates to reservation, sales, or similar fast-changing information. It is also used in data warehousing systems (under names like *star schema* and *snowflake schema*) where queries on big tables can do their initial work using the compact IDs, and only retrieve the bulky string data at the final stage (say, after you've decided which customers should receive an advertisement, and now you need to get their addresses).

Denormalization is when the pendulum swings the other way, and you find that for convenience or performance it's better to have fewer tables with more columns. Perhaps you receive data all bundled together in a format that would take too long to reorganize. Or you're recording events in real time, and it's easier to store a value like the browser "user agent" string verbatim rather than figuring out that this is browser number such-and-such and storing the corresponding ID number. This technique is mainly used in data warehouse systems.

Impala can work just fine in either paradigm. When data is normalized, join queries cross-reference data from multiple tables, with Impala automatically deducing the most efficient way to parallelize the work across the cluster. (See "Deep Dive: Joins and the Role of Statistics" on page 69 for a demonstration of how to optimize your join queries.) With the Parquet file format, you can use normalized or denormalized data. Parquet uses a column-oriented layout, which avoids the performance overhead normally associated with *wide tables* (those with many columns). The compression and encoding of Parquet data minimizes storage overhead for repeated values.

File Formats

You can use different file formats for Impala data files, similar to the notion of storage engines or special kinds of tables in other database systems. Some file formats are more convenient to produce, such as human-readable text. Others are more compact because of compression, or faster for data-warehouse-style queries because of column-oriented layout. The key advantage for Impala is that each file format is open, documented, and can be written and read by multiple Hadoop components, rather than being a "black box" where the data can only be accessed by custom-built software. So you can pick the best tool for each job: collecting data (typically with Sqoop and Flume), transforming it as it moves through the data pipeline (typically with Pig or Hive), and analyzing it with SQL queries (Impala, naturally) or programs written for frameworks such as Map-Reduce or Spark.

For this book, I'll focus on the two file formats that are polar opposites: text (most convenient and flexible) and Parquet (most compact and query-optimized). The other formats that Impala supports (Avro, RCFile, and SequenceFile) are ones you might be familiar with if your organization is already using Hadoop. But they are not optimized for the kinds of analytic queries that you do with Impala. If you're using Impala to produce data intended for use with analytic queries, use Parquet format for best results.

Text File Format

I'm always of two minds when talking about text format. It's the most familiar and convenient for beginners. It's the default file format for **CREATE TABLE** commands. It's very flexible, with a choice of delimiter characters. If you download freely available data sets, such as from a government agency, the data is probably in some sort of text format. You can create textual data files with a simple Unix command, or a Perl or Python script on any computer whether or not it's running Hadoop. You can fix format errors with any text editor. For small volumes of data, you can even do your own searches, sorts, and so on with simple Unix commands like grep, awk, and sort. Within Impala, you can change your mind at any time about whether a column is a STRING, INT, TINYINT, BIGINT, and so on. One minute you're summing numbers, the next you're doing SUBSTR() calls to check for leading zeros in a string, as illustrated in "Numbers Versus Strings" on page 91.

And yet, it's also the bulkiest format, thus the least efficient for serious Big Data applications. The number 1234567 takes up 7 bytes on disk; −1234567 takes up 8 bytes; −1234.567 takes up 9 bytes. The current date and time, such as 2014-07-09 15:31:01.409820000, takes up 29 bytes. When you're dealing with billions of rows, each unnecessary character represents gigabytes of wasted space on disk, and a proportional amount of wasted I/O, wasted memory, and wasted CPU cycles during queries.

Therefore, I'm going to advise again and again to prefer Parquet tables over text tables wherever practical. The column-oriented layout and compact storage format, with compression added on top, make Parquet the obvious choice when you are dealing with Big-Data-scale volume.

These examples demonstrate creating tables for text data files. Depending on the format of the input data, we specify different delimiter characters with the rather lengthy ROW FORMAT clause. STORED AS TEXTFILE is optional because that is the default format for **CREATE TABLE**. The default separator character is hex 01 (ASCII Ctrl-A), a character you're unlikely to find or enter by accident in textual data.

```
CREATE TABLE text_default_separator
  (c1 STRING, c2 STRING, c3 STRING);

CREATE TABLE text_including_stored_as_clause
  (c1 STRING, c2 STRING, c3 STRING) STORED AS TEXTFILE;

CREATE TABLE csv (c1 STRING, c2 STRING, c3 STRING)
  ROW FORMAT DELIMITED FIELDS TERMINATED BY "," STORED AS TEXTFILE;

CREATE TABLE tsv (c1 STRING, c2 STRING, c3 STRING)
  ROW FORMAT DELIMITED FIELDS TERMINATED BY "\t" STORED AS TEXTFILE;

CREATE TABLE psv (c1 STRING, c2 STRING, c3 STRING)
  ROW FORMAT DELIMITED FIELDS TERMINATED BY "|" STORED AS TEXTFILE;
```

Parquet File Format

The Parquet file format, which originated from collaboration between Twitter and Cloudera, is optimized for data-warehouse-style queries. Let's explore what that means and how it affects you as a developer.

Parquet is a binary file format. Numeric values are represented with consistent sizes, packed into a small number of bytes (either 4 or 8) depending on the range of the type. TIMESTAMP values are also represented in relatively few bytes. BOOLEAN values are packed into a single bit, rather than the strings true and false as in a text table. So all else being equal, a Parquet file is smaller than the equivalent text file.

But Parquet has other tricks up its sleeve. If the same value is repeated over and over, Parquet uses *run-length encoding* to condense that sequence down to two values: the value that's repeated, and how many times it's repeated. If a column has a modest number of different values, up to 16K, Parquet uses *dictionary encoding* for that column: it makes up numeric IDs for the values and stores those IDs in the data file along with one copy of the values, rather than repeating the values over and over. This automatically provides space reduction if you put denormalized data straight into Parquet. For example, if a data file contains a million rows, and each has one column with a state name such as California or Mississippi, the data file is essentially the same whether you convert those strings to state #1, #2, and so on and store the numbers, or if you let Parquet's dictionary encoding come up with the numeric IDs behind the scenes. The limit of 16K distinct values applies to each data file, so if your address table has more than 16K city names, but the table is partitioned by state so that the California cities are in one data file and the Mississippi cities are in a different data file, each data file could still use dictionary encoding for the CITY column.

See "Tutorial: The Journey of a Billion Rows" on page 51 for a demonstration of how much space you can save with Parquet format when all the compression and encoding techniques are combined.

Parquet is a column-oriented format. This means that the data for all values in a column are arranged physically adjacent to each other on disk. This technique speeds up certain kinds of queries that do not need to examine or retrieve all the columns, but do need to examine all or most of the values from particular columns:

```
-- The query can read all the values of a column without having to
-- read (and ignore) the values of the other columns in each row.
SELECT c3 FROM t1;

-- Analytic queries are always counting, summing, averaging and so on
-- columns for sales figures, web site visitors, sensor readings, and so on.
-- Those computations are nice and fast when no unnecessary data is read.
-- In this example, the query only needs to read C1 and C5, skipping all
-- other columns.
SELECT count(DISTINCT c1), sum(c1), max(c1), min(c1), avg(c1)
  FROM t1 WHERE c5 = 0;

-- Here we cross-reference columns from two different tables, along
-- with an ID column that is common to both. Again, the query only reads
-- values from the exact columns that are needed, making join queries
-- practical for tables in the terabyte and petabyte range.
SELECT attr01, attr15, attr37, name, email FROM
  visitor_details JOIN contact_info USING (visitor_id)
  WHERE year_joined BETWEEN 2005 AND 2010;
```

Column-oriented data is a popular feature in specialized data warehouse systems. For Impala, the column-oriented file format is just a small piece of the value proposition. The file format itself is open, so you can always get data in or out of it. Parquet files are readable and writable by many Hadoop components, so you can set up an ETL pipeline to use Parquet all the way through rather than starting in one format and converting to another at the end.

People commonly assume that the Parquet column-oriented format means each column is stored in a different data file. Not so! Each Parquet data file contains all the columns for a group of rows, but the values from each column are laid out next to each other within that file. When Impala needs to read all the values from a particular Parquet column, it seeks to a designated spot in the file and reads forward from there. The performance benefits of Parquet increase as you add more columns; for example, with 100 columns, a query only needs to read roughly 1% of each data file for each column referenced in the query.

Getting File Format Information

The **SHOW TABLE STATS** statement provides the basic information about the file format of the table, and each individual partition where appropriate:

```
[localhost:21000] > show table stats csv;
+-------+--------+------+--------------+--------+
| #Rows | #Files | Size | Bytes Cached | Format |
+-------+--------+------+--------------+--------+
| -1    | 1      | 58B  | NOT CACHED   | TEXT   |
+-------+--------+------+--------------+--------+
```

The **DESCRIBE FORMATTED** statement dumps a lot of information about each table, including any delimiter and escape characters specified for text tables:

```
[localhost:21000] > describe formatted csv;
...
| Storage Desc Params: | NULL                  | NULL |
|                      | field.delim           | ,    |
|                      | serialization.format  | ,    |
+----------------------+-----------------------+------+
```

Switching File Formats

Your preferred file format might change over time, after you conduct benchmarking experiments, or because of changes earlier in your ETL pipeline. Impala preserves the flexibility to change a table's file format at any time: simply replace the data with a new set of data files and run an **ALTER TABLE ... SET FILEFORMAT** statement. Or, for a partitioned table, you can leave older partitions in the previous file format, and use the new file format only for newer partitions.

This example demonstrates how to clone the structure of an existing table, switch the file format of the new table, and then copy data from the old to the new table. The data is converted to the new format during the copy operation.

```
CREATE TABLE t2 LIKE t1;
-- Copy the data, preserving the original file format.
INSERT INTO t2 SELECT * FROM t1;
ALTER TABLE t2 SET FILEFORMAT = PARQUET;
```

```
-- Now reload the data, this time converting to Parquet.
INSERT OVERWRITE t2 SELECT * FROM t1;
```

The following example demonstrates how a partitioned table could start off with one file format, but newly added partitions are switched to a different file format. Queries that access more than one partition automatically accommodate the file format for each partition.

```
CREATE TABLE t3 (c1 INT, c2 STRING, c3 TIMESTAMP)
  PARTITIONED BY (state STRING, city STRING);
ALTER TABLE t3 ADD PARTITION
  (state = 'CA', city = 'San Francisco');
-- Load some text data into this partition...
ALTER TABLE t3 ADD PARTITION
  (state = 'CA', city = 'Palo Alto');
-- Load some text data into this partition...
ALTER TABLE t3 ADD PARTITION
  (state = 'CA', city = 'Berkeley');
ALTER TABLE t3 PARTITION
  (state = 'CA', city = 'Berkeley')
  SET FILEFORMAT = PARQUET;
-- Load some Parquet data into this partition...
```

Aggregation

Aggregation is a general term meaning to take many small items and combine them into fewer larger ones. In the Impala context, aggregation is generally a positive thing. It comes up in several different contexts: you aggregate table data through aggregation functions and GROUP BY clauses; you deal with cluster resources such as memory and disk capacity by considering the total (aggregate) capacity, not the capacity of a single machine; and for performance reasons, sometimes you aggregate small files into larger ones.

When Impala queries are distributed to run across all the data nodes in a Hadoop cluster, in effect, the cluster acts like a single giant computer. For example, on a 100-node cluster, the memory and CPU power available for the query are 100 times as much as on a single server. We refer to this capacity using terms such as *aggregate memory*. That is why when you see that a resource-intensive workload requires many gigabytes of memory, that is not cause for alarm if you have a reasonably sized cluster of reasonably powerful servers.

For information about the memory consequences of aggregation queries, see "Optimizing Memory Usage" on page 37.

For discussion of aggregating (or coalescing) small files, see "Anti-Pattern: A Million Little Pieces" on page 79.

## CHAPTER 4

Common Developer Tasks for Impala

Here are the special Impala aspects of some standard operations familiar to database developers.

Getting Data into an Impala Table

Because Impala's feature set is oriented toward high-performance queries, much of the data you work with in Impala will originate from some other source, and Impala takes over near the end of the extract-transform-load (ETL) pipeline.

To get data into an Impala table, you can point Impala at data files in an arbitrary HDFS location; move data files from somewhere in HDFS into an Impala-managed directory; or copy data from one Impala table to another. Impala can query the original raw data files, without requiring any conversion or reorganization. Impala can also assist with converting and reorganizing data when those changes are helpful for query performance.

As a developer, you might be setting up all parts of a data pipeline, or you might work with files that already exist. Either way, the last few steps in the pipeline are the most important ones from the Impala perspective. You want the data files to go into a well-understood and predictable location in HDFS, and then Impala can work with them.

 See Chapter 5 for some demonstrations of ways to construct and load data for your own testing. You can do basic functional testing with trivial amounts of data. For performance and scalability testing, you'll need many gigabytes worth.

The following sections are roughly in order from the easiest techniques to the most complex. Once you have an ETL pipeline set up or a substantial amount of data loaded into Impala, you can explore all the different techniques and settle on one or two ingestion methods that work the best for you.

INSERT Statement

The **INSERT ... SELECT** statement is very simple to use, but requires you to have some existing data in an Impala table. You issue an **INSERT ... SELECT** statement to copy data from one table to another. You can convert the data to a different file format in the destination table, filter the data using **WHERE** clauses, and transform values using operators and built-in functions. With this technique, you can improve query efficiency by reorganizing the data in various ways; you'll see examples in following sections.

The **INSERT** statement can add data to an existing table with the **INSERT INTO** *table_name* syntax, or replace the entire contents of a table or partition with the **INSERT OVERWRITE** *table_name* syntax. Because Impala does not currently have **UPDATE** or **DELETE** statements, overwriting a table is how you make a change to existing data.

For First-Time Users Only

As you'll see in Chapter 5, you can issue an **INSERT ... VALUES** statement to create new data from literals and function return values. You can insert multiple rows through a single statement by including multiple tuples after the VALUES clause. We recommend against relying on this technique for production data, because it really only applies to very small volumes of data. Each **INSERT** statement produces a new tiny data file, which is a very inefficient layout for Impala queries against HDFS data. On the other hand, if you're entirely new to Hadoop, this is a simple way to get started and experiment with SQL syntax and various table layouts, data types, and file formats. You should expect to outgrow the **INSERT ... VALUES** syntax relatively quickly. You might graduate from tables with a few dozen rows straight to billions of rows when you start working with real data. Make sure to clean up any unneeded tables full of small files after finishing with **INSERT ... VALUES** experiments.

LOAD DATA Statement

If you have data files somewhere in HDFS already, you can issue a **LOAD DATA** statement to move data files in HDFS into the Impala data directory for a table.

Specify the HDFS path of a single file or a directory full of files. Impala moves the files out of their original location, to a directory under Impala's control. You don't need to know the destination directory; that aspect is managed by Impala. The Impala table or partition must already exist.

The files are not changed in any way by the **LOAD DATA** operation. They keep the same names, contents, and they all reside in the same destination directory.

This technique is most useful when you already have some sort of ETL pipeline that puts data files in a central HDFS location, and when Impala is the main consumer for the data. For example, you might use this technique if the final stage of your ETL process converts raw data files to query-optimized Parquet files. Leave the original data files where they are, and use **LOAD DATA** to move the corresponding Parquet files into the Impala directory structure for querying.

If you drop the table, the files are removed from HDFS. (The removed files are stored temporarily in the HDFS trashcan before being permanently deleted, so you can still recover them for some time after the **DROP TABLE**.)

External Tables

The **CREATE EXTERNAL TABLE** statement acts almost as a symbolic link, pointing Impala to a directory full of HDFS files. This is a handy technique to avoid copying data when other Hadoop components are already using the data files.

The statement begins with **CREATE EXTERNAL TABLE** statement and ends with the LOCATION _hdfs_path_ clause. The data files are not moved or changed at all. Thus, this operation is very quick, regardless of the size of the underlying data.

The files can still be added to or replaced by Hadoop components outside of Impala. (Issue a **REFRESH** table_name statement afterward if so.)

If you subsequently drop the table, the files are left untouched.

> This is a good technique to use if you have a robust system for managing incoming data in HDFS. For example, you might put the files in a central, well-known location to analyze the same data files through multiple SQL engines, NoSQL engines, or Hadoop components.

Figuring Out Where Impala Data Resides

All the techniques up to this point work without requiring you to specify any Impala-specific HDFS paths. Subsequent techniques require that you know the actual destination path in HDFS, based on the directory structure of tables managed by Impala. Here are techniques you can use to understand the overall Impala data directory structure, and to find the HDFS location of any Impala table or partition:

- Use the **DESCRIBE FORMATTED** statement in `impala-shell` to figure out the HDFS path corresponding to any Impala table. The path is shown in the `Location:` attribute.

- If some of your data resides outside the Impala table directories, you might use Linux commands such as `hdfs dfs -ls` *path* to browse around the HDFS directory structure to find the paths to specify for the **LOAD DATA** statement.

- Partitioned tables consist of multiple levels of directories, one level for each partition key column. To see that structure at a glance, use `hdfs dfs -du` *hdfs_path* to see the directory structure of all the partitions.

Manually Loading Data Files into HDFS

When your data files originate on your local Unix system, you can use Hadoop utilities to copy those files to specific locations within HDFS. The commands start with either `hdfs dfs` or `hadoop fs`, followed by arguments such as `-put`, `-ls`, `-du`, and others corresponding to familiar Unix utilities. The difference between `hdfs dfs` and `hadoop fs` is too subtle to matter (*http://bit.ly/1qKhyhQ*) for the examples in this book, so I typically use `hdfs dfs`.

If you are not already familiar with the HDFS directory structure, first learn how to check the HDFS path corresponding to an Impala table or partition ("Figuring Out Where Impala Data Resides" on page 29). See the tutorial using a billion rows of sample data ("Tutorial: The Journey of a Billion Rows" on page 51) for an example of this process.

When Parquet files come into HDFS for the first time, or are copied from one HDFS location to another, make sure to preserve the original block size. Rather than `hdfs dfs -put`, use the Linux command `hadoop distcp -pb` as follows:

```
hadoop distcp -pb local_source_file hdfs_destination_path
```

Hive

If you're already using batch-oriented SQL-on-Hadoop technology through the Apache Hive component, you can reuse Hive tables and their data directly in Impala without any time-consuming loading or conversion step. (This cross-compatibility applies to Hive tables that use Impala-compatible types for all columns.) Because Impala and Hive tables are interchangeable, after data is loaded through Hive, you can query it through Impala. This technique is for organizations that already have a Hadoop data pipeline set up. The steps are:

1. Do any **CREATE TABLE** statements either in Impala or through the Hive shell.

2. Do long-running **INSERT** statements through the Hive shell. Hive is well-suited for batch data transfer jobs that take many hours or even days.

3. In impala-shell, issue a one-time **INVALIDATE METADATA** *table_name* statement to make Impala aware of a table created through Hive.

4. In impala-shell, issue a **REFRESH** *table_name* statement any time data is added to or removed from a table through Hive or manual HDFS operations.

Sqoop

If you have data in another database system, such as an OLTP system or a data warehouse with limited capacity, you can bring it into Impala for large-scale analytics using Apache Sqoop.

The commands you run are sqoop-import or sqoop-import-all-tables. You specify user credentials and a JDBC-style URL to connect to the database system. Specify the options --null-string '\\N' and --null-non-string '\\N' to translate NULL values to the notation that Impala expects. (Due to the handling of escape sequences in the Linux shell, you typically have to specify the argument with double backslashes, '\\N'.)

The output is in the form of text, Avro, or SequenceFile data files. The Sqoop commands can also create the relevant SQL tables, and load those data files into the tables in HDFS.

If you create tables and load the data through Sqoop, afterward you issue **INVALIDATE METADATA** and/or **REFRESH** statements in Impala, the same as when you do those operations through Hive.

For general information about the Sqoop commands, see the Sqoop documentation (*http://sqoop.apache.org/docs/1.4.4/SqoopUserGuide.html*). For tutorial-style instructions, see the *Apache Sqoop Cookbook* by Ting and Cecho (O'Reilly); recipes 2.5 and 2.10 are especially helpful for using Sqoop with Impala.

Kite

The Kite SDK includes a command-line interface that can go directly from a text-based CSV file into a Parquet or Avro table in HDFS. After creating the table and loading the data through Kite, you issue **INVALIDATE METADATA** and/or **REFRESH** statements in Impala, the same as when you do those operations through Hive.

For instructions to download and use the Kite command-line interface, see the Kite documentation (*http://kitesdk.org/docs/current/guide*).

Porting SQL Code to Impala

For the most part, standard SQL that you bring over to Impala should run unchanged. The following aspects might require changes in the SQL code:

- Impala might not have every data type found on other database systems, or the name might be different. For example, Impala uses STRING as the type where other systems would use VARCHAR or CHAR.

- DDL statements have a number of Impala-specific or Hadoop-themed clauses. Expect to make changes to all your **CREATE TABLE** and **ALTER TABLE** statements.

- Because Impala has limited DML statements (for example, no **UPDATE** or **DELETE**), and no transactional statements (such as **COMMIT** or **ROLLBACK**), you might need to remove some statements from your code entirely. Most changes to data are performed by **INSERT INTO** or **INSERT OVERWRITE** statements in Impala.

- Queries use standard SQL-92 syntax. Some specific features are not supported, or are supported starting in a particular Impala release:

  — Every vendor has its own set of built-in functions. Impala supports a broad set of string, numeric, and date/time functions, but you'll need to cross-check against the ones used in your own code.

  — Impala is a little stricter than you might be used to in terms of casting and implicit conversions between types, in order to avoid unexpected loss of precision. Be ready to add some CAST() calls when working with expressions or columns of different types.

  — See "Recent Additions" on page 14 to see the latest enhancements to SQL portability.

See the Impala documentation (*http://bit.ly/porting-sql-impala*) for more on the subject of porting, including the most recent feature support.

Using Impala from a JDBC or ODBC Application

Although this book mainly emphasizes how the SQL language in Impala frees developers from having to write Java or other non-SQL programs for data processing, this section explains how to interface Java, C, PHP, and other kinds of applications with Impala through the standard JDBC interface. Driving Impala through these interfaces lets you operate the main program and display results on a non-Linux system such as a Mac OS X or Windows machine, or even a web page.

The best use case for this technique is in query-intensive applications. Data loading and ETL are relatively straightforward in SQL or in separate applications running directly on the server. Although it might be tempting to use the **INSERT ... VALUES** syntax from

JDBC or ODBC, remember that inserting rows one or a few at a time results in a very inefficient file layout for Impala (many small files) when it comes time to run queries.

Along the same lines, look for opportunities to run heavy-duty queries on large amounts of data through Impala. Although you can run simple "point queries" that look up a single row through Impala, that technique is really only efficient when the underlying data is pulled from tables stored in HBase, not HDFS. You typically write an Impala application to churn through huge quantities of sales, web traffic, bioscience, or similar data and render the results in graphs. Or you might have a web page that runs a query through PHP to retrieve a chunk of personalized information to display for a visitor. You would probably not use Impala as the backend for a web page that ran 50 queries to pull individual page elements out of a SQL table.

Make sure to always close query handles when finished. Because Impala runs queries against such big tables, there is often a significant amount of memory tied up during a query, which is important to release. Likewise, features like admission control and YARN resource management can limit the number of queries that run concurrently; if "zombie" queries hang around due to unclosed query handles in applications, the system can stop accepting new queries.

 I refer you to the official documentation and download sources for JDBC and ODBC driver information, because the details change periodically as new drivers are released.

JDBC

From Java, you can connect using the standard Hadoop JDBC driver (known as the Hive JDBC driver), and interface with Impala queries and result sets using standard JDBC API calls. See the Impala JDBC documentation (*http://bit.ly/impala-jdbc*) for details, such as the class name and the connection string for your particular security configuration.

ODBC

From C, C++, PHP, or other languages that support an ODBC interface, you can connect using a special Impala ODBC driver and go through standard ODBC API calls. See the Impala ODBC documentation (*http://bit.ly/impala-odbc*) for details.

From Python, you can use the pyodbc package (*https://code.google.com/p/pyodbc*) to issue SQL statements and get back the results as native Python data structures.

Using Impala with a Scripting Language

You can write a Python, Perl, Bash, or other kind of script that uses the features of those languages without delving into any database-specific APIs. You can use a script to produce or manipulate input data for Impala, and to drive the `impala-shell` interpreter to run SQL statements (primarily queries) and save or process the results.

 For serious application development, you can access database-centric APIs from a variety of scripting languages. See discussions of the `impyla` package for Python ("The impyla Package for Python Scripting" on page 35), and JDBC and ODBC connectivity options ("Using Impala from a JDBC or ODBC Application" on page 32) usable from many different languages.

Running Impala SQL Statements from Scripts

To execute SQL statements without any additional software prerequisites or API layers, run the `impala-shell` command with some command-line options. Specify the `-q` option to run a single SQL statement, or the `-f` option to process a file full of SQL statements. Typically, you also use the `-B` option to suppress the ASCII art boxes around query results, which makes the textual output easier to consume.

Variable Substitution

The `impala-shell` interpreter doesn't currently have a built-in way to do variable substitution. The typical way to substitute variables is to embed the SQL statements in a shell script, like so:

```
#!/bin/bash

export DB_NAME=tpc
export TABLE_NAME=customer_address
export CRITERIA=Oakland
export CUTOFF=20

impala-shell -d $DB_NAME <<EOF
select * from $DB_NAME.$TABLE_NAME where ca_city = '$CRITERIA' limit $CUTOFF;
EOF

...more shell code...
```

For more about the `impala-shell` options to control output format, see "Tutorial: Verbose and Quiet impala-shell Output" on page 88.

Saving Query Results

The `-o` *filename* option of the `impala-shell` command saves the output in a file. You typically use `-o` in combination with `-q` or `-f` to run a single query or a file of SQL commands, then exit. To make the output easier to parse, also use the `-B` option to suppress the ASCII art boxes around query results, and optionally the `--output_delimiter=character` option to format the output with a comma, pipe, or some other character as the separator.

The `-o` option saves the `impala-shell` output in the local filesystem. To save results in HDFS, you put the result rows into an Impala table using SQL syntax such as `CREATE TABLE AS SELECT` or `INSERT ... SELECT`. You can set up the table with the desired characteristics of file format (`STORED AS` clause), separator character for text files (`ROW FORMAT` clause), and HDFS path for the output files (`LOCATION` clause).

The impyla Package for Python Scripting

The many scientific libraries available for Python make it a popular choice for data scientists to code in. The `impyla` package (still under development) acts as a bridge between the Python database API and the protocol that Impala supports for its JDBC and ODBC drivers. The Python programs use the Python DB API 2.0, from the PEP-249 specification.

For example, here is a script that issues a **SHOW TABLES** statement to get a list of tables in the `DEFAULT` database, then **DESCRIBE** statements to get details about the structure of each table, and then issues queries to get the number of rows in each table. The result sets come back as lists of tuples. Substitute your own hostname here, but keep the same port, `21050`, where Impala listens for JDBC requests. You can run scripts like this on all kinds of systems—not only on Linux machines with Hadoop installed; this particular script was executed on Mac OS X.

```
from impala.dbapi import connect

conn = connect(host='a1730.abcde.example.com', port=21050)
try:
  cur = conn.cursor()
  try:
    cur.execute('show tables in default')
    tables_in_default_db = cur.fetchall()
    print tables_in_default_db
    for table in tables_in_default_db:
      print "Table: " + table[0]
      try:
        cur.execute('describe `%s`' % (table[0]))
        table_layout = cur.fetchall()
        for row in table_layout:
          print "Column: " + row[0] + ", type: " + row[1] + ", comment: " + row[2]
```

```
    except:
      print "Error describing table " + table[0]
    cur.execute('select count(*) from `%s`' % (table[0]))
    result = cur.fetchall()
    count = str(result[0][0])
    print "Rows = " + count
  except:
    print "Error getting list of tables."
  cur.close()
except:
  print "Error establishing connection to Impala."
```

In addition to writing Python programs that call into Impala, you can write simple UDFs in Python through impyla, ship the resulting binaries from a development machine to your Impala cluster, and the functions from Impala queries. To use this capability, you need certain other software prerequisites on the development machine (for example, LLVM) and should be familiar with the data types used in C++ UDFs for Impala.

See the impyla introduction blog post (*http://blog.cloudera.com/blog/2014/04/a-new-python-client-for-impala*) and the impyla Github repo (*https://github.com/cloudera/impyla*) for details and examples. impyla also includes some features that integrate with the pandas analytical package for Python (*https://pypi.python.org/pypi/pandas/0.13.1*).

Optimizing Impala Performance

If you come from a traditional database background, you might have engraved in your mind the notion that indexes are crucial for query speed. If your experience extends to data warehousing environments, you might be comfortable with the idea of doing away with indexes, because it's often more efficient when doing heavy duty analysis to just scan the entire table or certain partitions.

Impala embraces this data warehousing approach of avoiding indexes by not having any indexes at all. After all, data files can be added to HDFS at any time by components other than Impala. Index maintenance would be very expensive. The HDFS storage subsystem is optimized for fast reads of big chunks of data. So the types of queries that can be expensive in a traditional database system are standard operating procedure for Impala, as long as you follow the best practices for performance.

Having said that, the laws of physics still apply, and if there is a way for a query to read, evaluate, and transmit less data overall, of course the query will be proportionally faster as a result. With Impala, the biggest I/O savings come from using partitioned tables and choosing the most appropriate file format. The most complex and resource-intensive queries tend to involve join operations, and the critical factor there is to collect statistics (using the **COMPUTE STATS** statement) for all the tables involved in the join.

The following sections give some guidelines for optimizing performance and scalability for queries and overall memory usage. For those who prefer to learn by doing, later sections show examples and tutorials for file formats ("Tutorial: The Journey of a Billion Rows" on page 51), partitioned tables ("Making a Partitioned Table" on page 64), and join queries and table statistics ("Deep Dive: Joins and the Role of Statistics" on page 69).

Optimizing Query Performance

The most resource-intensive and performance-critical Impala queries tend to be joins: pulling together related data from multiple tables. For all tables involved in join queries, issue a **COMPUTE STATS** statement after loading initial data into a table, or adding new data that changes the table size by 30% or more.

When a table has a column or set of columns that's almost always used for filtering, such as date or geographic region, consider partitioning that table by that column or columns. Partitioning allows queries to analyze the rows containing specific values of the partition key columns, and avoid reading partitions with irrelevant data.

At the end of your ETL process, you want the data to be in a file format that is efficient for data-warehouse-style queries. In practice, Parquet format is the most efficient for Impala. Other binary formats such as Avro are also more efficient than delimited text files.

See "Tutorial: The Journey of a Billion Rows" on page 51 for a sequence of examples that explores all these aspects of query tuning. For more background information, see the related discussions of joins and statistics ("Deep Dive: Joins and the Role of Statistics" on page 69), file formats ("File Formats" on page 21) including Parquet ("Parquet Files: The Biggest Blocks of All" on page 16), and partitioning ("Working with Partitioned Tables" on page 39).

Optimizing Memory Usage

This section provides guidelines and strategies for keeping memory use low. Efficient use of memory is important for overall performance, and also for scalability in a highly concurrent production setup.

For many kinds of straightforward queries, Impala uses a modest and predictable amount of memory, regardless of the size of the table. As intermediate results become available from different nodes in the cluster, the data is sent back to the coordinator node rather than being buffered in memory. For example, SELECT *column_list* FROM *table* or SELECT *column_list* FROM *table* WHERE *conditions* both read data from disk using modestly sized read buffers, regardless of the volume of data or the HDFS block size.

Certain kinds of clauses increase the memory requirement. For example, ORDER BY involves sorting intermediate results on remote nodes. (Although in Impala 1.4 and later, the maximum memory used by ORDER BY is lower than in previous releases, and very large sort operations write to a work area on disk to keep memory usage under control.) GROUP BY involves building in-memory data structures to keep track of the intermediate result for each group. UNION and DISTINCT also build in-memory data structures to prune duplicate values.

The size of the additional work memory does depend on the amount and types of data in the table. Luckily, you don't need all this memory on any single machine, but rather spread across all the data nodes of the cluster.

Calls to aggregation functions such as MAX(), AVG(), and SUM() reduce the size of the overall data. The working memory for those functions themselves is proportional to the number of groups in the GROUP BY clause. For example, computing SUM() for an entire table involves very little memory because only a single variable is needed to hold the intermediate sum. Using SUM() in a query with GROUP BY year involves one intermediate variable corresponding to each year, presumably not many different values. A query calling an aggregate function with GROUP BY unique_column could have millions or billions of different groups, where the time and memory to compute all the different aggregate values could be substantial.

The UNION operator does more work than the UNION ALL operator, because UNION collects the values from both sides of the query and then eliminates duplicates. Therefore, if you know there will be no duplicate values, or there is no harm in having duplicates, use UNION ALL instead of UNION.

The LIMIT clause puts a cap on the number of results, allowing the nodes performing the distributed query to skip unnecessary processing. If you know you need a maximum of N results, include a LIMIT N clause so that Impala can return the results faster.

A GROUP BY clause involving a STRING column is much less efficient than with a numeric column. This is one of the cases where it makes sense to normalize data, replacing long or repeated string values with numeric IDs.

Although INT is the most familiar integer type, if you are dealing with values that fit into smaller ranges (such as 1–12 for month and 1–31 for day), specifying the "smallest" appropriate integer type means the hash tables, intermediate result sets, and so on will use 1/2, 1/4, or 1/8 as much memory for the data from those columns. Use the other integer types (TINYINT, SMALLINT, and BIGINT) when appropriate based on the range of values.

You can also do away with separate time-based fields in favor of a single TIMESTAMP column. The EXTRACT() function lets you pull out the individual fields when you need them.

Although most of the Impala memory considerations revolve around queries, inserting into a Parquet table (especially a partitioned Parquet table) can also use substantial memory. Up to 1 GB of Parquet data is buffered in memory before being written to disk.

With a partitioned Parquet table, there could be 1 GB of memory used for each partition being inserted into, multiplied by the number of nodes in the cluster, multiplied again by the number of cores on each node.

Use one of the following techniques to minimize memory use when writing to Parquet tables:

- Impala can determine when an **INSERT** ... **SELECT** into a partitioned table is especially memory-intensive and redistribute the work to avoid excessive memory usage. For this optimization to be effective, you must issue a **COMPUTE STATS** statement for the source table where the data is being copied from, so that Impala can make a correct estimate of the volume and distribution of data being inserted.

- If statistics are not available for the source table, or the automatic memory estimate is inaccurate, you can force lower memory usage for the **INSERT** statement by including the [SHUFFLE] hint immediately before the SELECT keyword in the **INSERT** ... **SELECT** statement.

- Running a separate **INSERT** statement for each partition minimizes the number of memory buffers allocated at any one time. In the **INSERT** statement, include a clause PARTITION(*col1=val1,col2=val2,* ...) to specify constant values for all the partition key columns.

Working with Partitioned Tables

In Impala, as in large-scale data warehouse systems, the primary way for a schema designer to speed up queries is to create partitioned tables. The data is physically divided based on all the different values in one column or a set of columns, known as the partition key columns. Partitioning acts like indexes, instead of looking up one row at a time from widely scattered items, the rows with identical partition keys are physically grouped together. Impala uses the fast bulk I/O capabilities of HDFS to read all the data stored in particular partitions, based on references to the partition key columns in WHERE or join clauses.

With Impala, partitioning is ready to go out of the box with no setup required. It's expected that practically every user will employ partitioning for their tables that truly qualify as Big Data.

Frequently tested columns like YEAR, COUNTRY, and so on make good partition keys. For example, if you partition on a YEAR column, all the data for a particular year can be physically placed together on disk. Queries with clauses such as WHERE YEAR = 1987 or WHERE YEAR BETWEEN 2006 AND 2009 can zero in almost instantly on the data to read, and then read that data very efficiently because all the rows are located adjacent to each other in a few large files.

Partitioning is great for reducing the overall amount of data to read, which in turn reduces the CPU cycles to test column values and the memory to hold intermediate results. All these reductions flow straight through to the bottom line: faster query performance. If you have 100 years worth of historical data, and you want to analyze only the data for 1 year, you can do that 100 times as fast with a partitioned table as with an unpartitioned one (all else being equal).

This section provides some general guidelines. For demonstrations of some of these techniques, see "Making a Partitioned Table" on page 64.

Finding the Ideal Granularity

Now that I have told you how partitioning makes your queries faster, let's look at some design aspects for partitioning in Impala (or Hadoop in general). Sometimes, taking an existing partitioned table from a data warehouse and reusing the schema as-is isn't optimal for Impala.

Remember, Hadoop's HDFS filesystem does best with a relatively small number of big files. (By big, we mean in the range of 128 MB to 1 GB; ideally, nothing smaller than 64 MB.) If you partition on columns that are so fine-grained that each partition has very little data, the bulk I/O and parallel processing of Hadoop mostly goes to waste. Thus, often you'll find that an existing partitioning scheme needs to be reduced by one level to put sufficient data in each partition.

For example, if a table was partitioned by year, month, and day in pre-Hadoop days, you might get more efficient queries by partitioning only for year and month in Impala. Or if you have an older table partitioned by city and state, maybe a more efficient layout for Impala is only partitioned by state (or even by region). From the Hadoop point of view, it's not much different to read a 40 MB partition than it is to read a 20 MB one, and reading only 5 MB is unlikely to see much advantage from Hadoop strengths like parallel execution. This is especially true if you frequently run reports that hit many different partitions, such as when you partition down to the day but then run reports for an entire month or a full year.

Inserting into Partitioned Tables

When you insert into a partitioned table, again Impala parallelizes that operation. If the data has to be split up across many different partitions, that means many data files being written to simultaneously, which can exceed limits on things like HDFS file descriptors. When you insert into Parquet tables, each data file being written requires a memory buffer equal to the Parquet block size, which by default is 1 GB for Impala. Thus, what seems like a relatively innocuous operation (copy 10 years of data into a table partitioned by year, month, and day) can take a long time or even fail, despite a low overall volume of information. Here again, it's better to work with big chunks of information at once. Impala **INSERT** syntax lets you work with one partition at a time:

```
CREATE TABLE raw_data
  (year SMALLINT, month TINYINT, c1 STRING, c2 INT, c3 BOOLEAN);
-- Load some data into this unpartitioned table...

CREATE TABLE partitioned_table (c1 STRING, c2 INT, c3 BOOLEAN)
  PARTITIONED BY (year SMALLINT, month TINYINT);
-- Copy data into the partitioned table, one partition at a time.
INSERT INTO partitioned_table PARTITION (year=2000, month=1)
  SELECT c1, c2, c3 FROM raw_data WHERE year=2000 AND month=1;
INSERT INTO partitioned_table PARTITION (year=2000, month=2)
  SELECT c1, c2, c3 FROM raw_data WHERE year=2000 AND month=2;
...
```

It's easy to write a query that generates a set of **INSERT** statements like this by finding all the distinct values for the partition key columns. Then you can run the resulting statements in a SQL script. For example:

```
SELECT DISTINCT
  concat('insert into partitioned_table partition (year=',
    cast(year as string),', month=',cast(month as string),
    ') select c1, c2, c3 from raw_data where year=',
    cast(year as string),' and month=',cast(month as string),';') AS command
  FROM raw_data;
+----------------------------------------------------------------...
| command                                                     ...
+----------------------------------------------------------------...
| insert into partitioned_table partition (year=2000, month=1) select ...
| insert into partitioned_table partition (year=2000, month=2) select ...
| insert into partitioned_table partition (year=2000, month=3) select ...
...
```

Pro Tip

When you run Impala queries to generate other SQL statements, start `impala-shell` with the `-B` option. That option suppresses the ASCII boxes around query results, making the output easier to redirect or copy and paste into a script file. See "Tutorial: Verbose and Quiet impala-shell Output" on page 88 for examples.

Adding and Loading New Partitions

One of the convenient aspects of Impala partitioned tables is that the partitions are just HDFS directories, where you can put data files without going through any file conversion or even Impala **INSERT** statements. In this example, you create the partitions individually and use the **LOAD DATA** statement or some mechanism outside Impala to ingest the data.

```
-- Set up empty partitions.
ALTER TABLE partitioned_table ADD PARTITION (year=2010, month=1);
ALTER TABLE partitioned_table ADD PARTITION (year=2010, month=2);
...
ALTER TABLE partitioned_table ADD PARTITION (year=2014, month=1);
ALTER TABLE partitioned_table ADD PARTITION (year=2014, month=2);
...

-- Move data that already exists in HDFS into appropriate partition directories.
LOAD DATA INPATH '/user/warehouse/this_year/january' INTO partitioned_table
  PARTITION (year=2014, month=1);
LOAD DATA INPATH '/user/warehouse/this_year/february' INTO partitioned_table
  PARTITION (year=2014, month=2);

-- Or tell Impala to look for specific partitions in specific HDFS directories.
ALTER TABLE partitioned_table PARTITION (year=2014, month=3)
  SET LOCATION '/user/warehouse/this_year/march';

-- If the files are not already in HDFS, shell out to an external command
-- that does 'hdfs dfs -put' or similar.
! load_projected_data_for_2020.sh
-- Make Impala aware of the files that were added by non-SQL means.
REFRESH partitioned_table;
```

See "Anti-Pattern: A Million Little Pieces" on page 79 for some other tricks you can use to avoid fragmentation and excessive memory use when inserting into partitioned Parquet tables.

Writing User-Defined Functions

If you have exotic algorithms or high-performance computations coded in C+\+ but you want users to go through a familiar SQL interface rather than you writing a whole C++ application, you can encapsulate the special code in a *user-defined function* (UDF), and call that function from SQL in the same way as a built-in Impala function.

For best performance, write any UDFs in C++; UDFs can also use a Java interface, but the option is primarily for reusing existing UDFs written for Hive.

Scalar UDFs produce a value for each input row, and are primarily for convenience and readability; you can bundle complex string processing or arithmetic operations into a single function call, possibly more efficient than building the same logic with a sequence of expressions within the query.

User-defined aggregate functions (UDAFs) are more complex. They return one or many values based on groups of related values from a table. If your analytic software relies on "secret sauce" algorithms that give you a competitive edge, you would likely implement those as UDAFs for Impala. (Because UDAFs build up their results over potentially millions or billions of calls to the same function, your pointer arithmetic and memory allocation need to be thoroughly debugged before executing the code inside Impala.)

Coding UDFs and UDAFs is beyond the scope of this book. For instructions for C++ and Java UDFs, see the Impala documentation (*http://bit.ly/impala-udfs*). For header files, build environment, and code examples, see the Impala UDF developer GitHub repository (*https://github.com/cloudera/impala/tree/master/be/src/udf_samples*).

You can also write simple UDFs in Python, using the impyla Python package ("The impyla Package for Python Scripting" on page 35).

Collaborating with Your Administrators

Although you can do a substantial amount of coding and testing in a purely development environment, at some point you will probably interact in some way with production systems where security policies and resource allocations are controlled by administrators. You might hand off queries, scripts, or JDBC applications to be run in a production environment. You might connect directly to a production system to run ad hoc queries. Or you might be in a *devops* role where you share both development and administration responsibilities.

Although the details of Impala administration are outside the scope of this book, here are some tips to help set expectations and smooth communications between you as a developer and the administrators in your organization.

It is common for database vendors to suggest allocating a high percentage of physical memory, often 80% or more, for exclusive use of database software. Impala also benefits from having access to large amounts of physical memory for processing intermediate results from clauses like joins, `ORDER BY`, and `GROUP BY`. On a development system, you might be spoiled by having exclusive access to all memory for all machines. Practice running all your SQL with memory limits that reflect how much RAM will be available to Impala in the production environment. Receiving "out of memory" errors typically means that you are missing statistics that help Impala to plan and distribute the work for the most resource-intensive queries, or that you should take other tuning steps to help the queries execute using less RAM.

Designing for Security

In a development environment, you might have wide-open access to all the data. In a production environment, access is likely controlled at the database, table, and even column level by the Sentry authorization system. Make life easier for administrators by grouping related tables logically into databases so that users can be granted privileges on all the tables in a database at once. Use consistent naming conventions for tables and columns to make it easier for an administrator to define views that access subsets of columns corresponding to the data that can be accessed by different classes of users. (For bonus points, create such views up front as part of your schema design process.) For example, in a healthcare organization, a table might contain some data that is only available to doctors, a different subset of information that is available to lab technicians, and yet another subset of information that is available to health insurance providers. Find out up front if your organization has already defined classes of users like these.

Understanding Resource Management

In addition to using these categories for security purposes, an administrator might use YARN and Impala's admission control feature to provide different proportions of cluster resources to different groups of users. The resource allocation policies help prioritize and schedule the work across different Hadoop components on a busy cluster, ensuring that everybody stays within their defined limits for overall RAM and CPU usage, and in Impala's case, the number of queries allowed to execute concurrently. Thus, be prepared to discuss whether queries for different types of users are more frequent, or more memory- and CPU-intensive than others to help administrators set up the resource allocation policies for a busy cluster. Understand the memory usage of particular queries and how that memory usage varies depending on the amount of data, because the production environment might have larger data volume than the development and test environment.

Helping to Plan for Performance (Stats, HDFS Caching)

No matter how well you design your schema and how efficient you make your queries, when your code goes into production, it might perform differently than in your dev/test environment. The cluster will likely be running other workloads at the same time —both Impala queries and non-Impala jobs. The volume of data in your tables might go up as new data arrives, or go down as older partitions are dropped.

Two important features to help your code perform well in an ever-changing environment are the **COMPUTE STATS** statement and HDFS caching.

The **COMPUTE STATS** statement gathers metadata that lets Impala optimize resource-intensive queries and insert operations, particularly join queries and **INSERT**s, into partitioned Parquet tables. The administrator might need to run **COMPUTE STATS** periodically whenever data volume in a table changes by a substantial amount. (Use 30% as a guideline, and then do your own testing to see how the explain plans for your join queries change depending on data volumes and the presence or absence of statistics.) Practice automating this step in any data-loading scripts you create. Communicate to your administrator all the tables involved in join queries, which are the most important ones when it comes to keeping the statistics up-to-date.

HDFS caching helps reduce I/O and memory-to-memory copying by keeping specified tables and partitions entirely in a special memory cache area. (The size of this cache does not count against the memory limits you can set for Impala.) The data is cached persistently, rather than being evicted each time new data is read. Therefore, it is suitable for frequently queried lookup tables, or tables and partitions that are being intensively queried during a particular timeframe. The administrator sets the size of the HDFS cache and divides it into cache pools with different characteristics for use by different classes of applications. Again, practice with this feature in your dev/test environment, and be prepared to discuss with your administrator which tables and partitions are most valuable to cache, and which cache pool they should go into. (The caching information can be set up with the initial **CREATE TABLE** statements, or applied later through **ALTER TABLE** statements.) The major benefit of this feature is scalability in a high-concurrency environment, so don't be discouraged if you don't see a big performance difference in a single-user test environment.

Understanding Cluster Topology

As a developer, you might work with a different cluster setup than is actually used in production. Here are some things to watch out for, to understand the performance and scalability implications as your application moves from a dev/test setup into production:

- For basic functional testing, you might use a single-node setup, perhaps running inside a virtual machine. You can check SQL compatibility, try out built-in functions, check data type compatibility and experiment with CAST(), see that your custom UDFs work correctly, and so on. (Perhaps with relatively small data volume, just to check correctness.)

- To see what happens with distributed queries, you could use a relatively small cluster, such as two or four nodes. This allows you to see some performance and scalability benefits from parallelizing the queries. On a dev/test cluster, the name node is probably on the same host as one of the data nodes, which is not a problem when the cluster is running under a light workload.

- For production, you'll probably have a separate host for the name node, and a substantial number of data nodes. Here, the chances of a node failing are greater. (In this case, rerun any queries that were in flight.) Or one node might experience a performance issue, dragging down the response time of queries. (This type of problem is best detected with monitoring software such as Cloudera Manager.) Also, this is the time to double-check the guideline about installing Impala on all the data nodes in the cluster (to avoid I/O slowdown due to remote reads) and only on the data nodes (to avoid using up memory and CPU unnecessarily on the name node, which has a lot of work to do on a busy cluster).

Always Close Your Queries

Because Impala queries can be resource-intensive, production deployments typically use strategies such as resource management and admission control to cap the number of concurrent queries at a level the cluster can comfortably accommodate. This is a constraint you might not face in a development environment. In an application that submits queries through an interface such as JDBC, ODBC, HiveServer2, or Beeswax, make sure that all queries are closed when finished. Address this aspect in all execution paths and error handling. Otherwise, your application could leave "zombie" unclosed queries that fill up the available execution slots and prevent other queries from running. If this happens, expect a call from your administrator.

## CHAPTER 5

Tutorials and Deep Dives

The following sections cover aspects of Impala that deserve a closer look. Brief examples illustrate interesting features for new users. More complex topics are covered by tutorials or deep dives into the inner workings.

Tutorial: From Unix Data File to Impala Table

Here is what your first Unix command-line session might look like when you're using Impala. This example from a Bash shell session creates a couple of text files (which could be named anything), copies those files into the HDFS filesystem, and points an Impala table at the data so that it can be queried through SQL. The exact HDFS paths might differ based on your HDFS configuration and Linux users.

```
$ cat >csv.txt
1,red,apple,4
2,orange,orange,4
3,yellow,banana,3
4,green,apple,4
^D
$ cat >more_csv.txt
5,blue,bubblegum,0.5
6,indigo,blackberry,0.2
7,violet,edible flower,0.01
8,white,scoop of vanilla ice cream,3
9,black,licorice stick,0.2
^D
$ hadoop fs -mkdir /user/hive/staging
$ hadoop fs -put csv.txt /user/hive/staging
$ hadoop fs -put more_csv.txt /user/hive/staging
```

Sometimes the user you are logged in as does not have permission to manipulate HDFS files. In that case, issue the commands with the permissions of the hdfs user, using the form:

```
sudo -u hdfs hadoop fs arguments
```

Now that the data files are in the HDFS filesystem, let's go into the Impala shell and start working with them. (Some of the prompts and output are abbreviated here for easier reading by first-time users.) This example creates a new database, in case this experiment turns into a project with a whole set of related tables. Then we create a table inside this database, move the data files into the table, and run some queries.

```
$ impala-shell
> create database food_colors;
> use food_colors;
> create table food_data
    (id int, color string, food string, weight float)
    row format delimited fields terminated by ',';
> -- Here's where we move the data files from an arbitrary
  -- HDFS location to under Impala control.
> load data inpath '/user/hive/staging' into table food_data;
Query finished, fetching results ...
+-------------------------------------------------------------+
| summary                                                     |
+-------------------------------------------------------------+
| Loaded 2 file(s). Total files in destination location: 2 |
+-------------------------------------------------------------+
> select food, color as "Possible Color" from food_data where
    food = 'apple';
Query finished, fetching results ...
+-------+----------------+
| food  | possible color |
+-------+----------------+
| apple | red            |
| apple | green          |
+-------+----------------+
Returned 2 row(s) in 0.66s
> select food as "Top 5 Heaviest Foods", weight
    from food_data
    order by weight desc limit 5;
Query finished, fetching results ...
+---------------------------+--------------------+
| top 5 heaviest foods      | weight             |
+---------------------------+--------------------+
| orange                    | 4                  |
| apple                     | 4                  |
| apple                     | 4                  |
| scoop of vanilla ice cream | 3                 |
| banana                    | 3                  |
+---------------------------+--------------------+
```

```
Returned 5 row(s) in 0.49s
> quit;
```

Back in the Unix shell, see how the **CREATE DATABASE** and **CREATE TABLE** statements created some new directories and how the **LOAD DATA** statement moved the original data files into an Impala-managed directory:

```
$ hadoop fs -ls -R /user/hive/warehouse/food_colors.db
drwxrwxrwt   - impala hive           0 2013-08-29 16:14 /user/h
ive/warehouse/food_colors.db/food_data
-rw-rw-rw-   3 hdfs   hive          66 2013-08-29 16:12 /user/h
ive/warehouse/food_colors.db/food_data/csv.txt
-rw-rw-rw-   3 hdfs   hive         139 2013-08-29 16:12 /user/h
ive/warehouse/food_colors.db/food_data/more_csv.txt
```

In one easy step, you've gone from a collection of human-readable text files to a SQL table that you can query using standard, widely known syntax. The data is automatically replicated and distributed across a cluster of networked machines by virtue of being put into an HDFS directory.

These same basic techniques scale up to enormous tables with billions of rows. By that point, you would likely be using a more compact and efficient data format than plain text files, and you might include a partitioning clause in the **CREATE TABLE** statement to split up the data files by date or category. Don't worry, you can easily upgrade your Impala tables and rearrange the data as you learn the more advanced Impala features. In fact, that's the subject of a later tutorial: "Tutorial: The Journey of a Billion Rows" on page 51.

Tutorial: Queries Without a Table

To understand how Impala works at the extreme ends of the spectrum, let's consider for a moment the least intensive queries we could run. Impala does not have a built-in trivial table like the DUAL table in Oracle. Instead, to get back a single-row result of an expression, you construct a query with all constant expressions or function calls in the SELECT list, and leave off the FROM clause. Here are sample queries for you to run in the impala-shell interpreter; see if you can predict the results:

```
SELECT 1;
SELECT "hello world";
SELECT 2+2;
SELECT 10 > 5;
SELECT now();
```

You can use this very valuable table-less **SELECT** technique for experimenting with the detailed semantics of Impala functions, data types and casting, NULL handling, and all kinds of expressions.

These examples illustrate numeric expressions and arithmetic:

```
SELECT 1 + 0.5;
SELECT 1 / 3;
SELECT 1e6, 1.5e6;
SELECT 30000 BETWEEN min_smallint() AND max_smallint();
+-----------------------------------------------+
| 30000 between min_smallint() and max_smallint() |
+-----------------------------------------------+
| true                                          |
+-----------------------------------------------+
```

 The results of those floating-point expressions are more precise in Impala 1.4 and later than in previous releases, due to the introduction of the DECIMAL type.

These examples illustrate type conversions:

```
SELECT cast(1e6 AS string);
SELECT cast(true AS string);
SELECT cast(99.44 AS int);
```

These examples illustrate what happens when NULL is used in various contexts:

```
SELECT 1 + NULL, 1 = NULL, 1 > NULL, NULL = NULL, NULL IS NULL;
SELECT cast(NULL AS STRING), cast(NULL AS BIGINT), cast(NULL AS BOOLEAN);
```

These examples illustrate string literals and string functions:

```
SELECT 'hello\nworld';
SELECT "abc\t012345\txyz";
SELECT concat('hello',NULL);
SELECT substr('hello',-2,2);
```

These examples illustrate regular expression comparisons and functions:

```
SELECT 'abc123xyz' REGEXP '[[:digit:]]{3}';
+-----------------------------------+
| 'abc123xyz' regexp '[[:digit:]]{3}' |
+-----------------------------------+
| true                              |
+-----------------------------------+

SELECT regexp_extract('>>>abc<<<','.*([a-z]+)',1);
+---------------------------------------------+
| regexp_extract('>>>abc<<<', '.*([a-z]+)', 1) |
+---------------------------------------------+
| abc                                         |
+---------------------------------------------+

SELECT regexp_replace('123456','(2|4|6)','x');
```

```
+-------------------------------------------+
| regexp_replace('123456', '(2|4|6)', 'x') |
+-------------------------------------------+
| 1x3x5x                                    |
+-------------------------------------------+
```

This example illustrates date/time expressions, functions, and arithmetic:

```
SELECT now() + INTERVAL 3 DAYS + INTERVAL 5 HOURS;
+-------------------------------------------+
| now() + interval 3 days + interval 5 hours |
+-------------------------------------------+
| 2014-08-03 16:48:44.201018000             |
+-------------------------------------------+
```

These types of queries can help you construct or debug the individual pieces of a complicated query. For example, you typically run a simple test to confirm that you have the right regex notation, function arguments, format strings, and so on, before applying a regular expression or date calculation to billions of rows.

Queries with no FROM clause are not subject to the limits imposed by the admission control feature on the number of concurrent queries; they are not parallelized and distributed across multiple cluster nodes. Instead, all work is done on the coordinator node. In terms of resource management, Impala still allocates a default amount of memory (several megabytes) for each such query, because even a query without a table might evaluate some enormously complicated expression or call a complex user-defined function.

Tutorial: The Journey of a Billion Rows

Now that we've seen how you can try out basic SQL features with no table or a tiny table, let's get serious. In the Big Data field, there's little point experimenting with thousands or even millions of rows. That volume of data is effectively the same as the smallest tables you could construct, so you don't really learn much about distributed queries or Impala performance.

Let's set up a table with a *billion* rows and see what we can learn. With a billion rows, by definition we'll be working with gigabytes of data. Any inefficiency or wasted storage will be easy to spot. Any query that processes those gigabytes in only a few seconds will be cause for celebration.

Generating a Billion Rows of CSV Data

First, let's generate a billion rows of general-purpose data. I intentionally chose an old-school technique, a simple Python script generating a single big file, to illustrate how Impala bridges the world of traditional Unix and databases, and the new Hadoop world of Big Data and distributed parallel computing.

```python
#! /usr/bin/python

"""
multicols.py: Generate an arbitrary number of rows with random values.
"""

import sys
from random import *

# ---
# Load a list of the biggest US cities (289 of them),
# to pick a random city/state combination for an address.

usa_cities = []

def load_cities():
  global usa_cities
  lines = [line.rstrip() for line in open("usa_cities.lst").readlines()]
  usa_cities = [line.split(",") for line in lines]

def random_city():
  if usa_cities == []:
    load_cities()
  which = randint(0,len(usa_cities)-1)
  return usa_cities[which]

if __name__ == '__main__':

# Produce text format data with different kinds of separators.
  possible_separators = { "pipe": "|", "comma": ",", "csv": ",",
    "ctrl-a": "\x01", "hash": "#", "bang": "!", "tab": "\t",
    "tsv": "\t" }

# Accept number of rows to generate as command-line argument.
  try:
    count = int(sys.argv[1])
  except:
    count = 1

# For random numeric values, define upper bound as another command-line argument.
# By default, values are 0-99999.
  try:
    upper = int(sys.argv[2])
  except:
    upper = 99999

# Accept mnemonic for separator characters as command-line argument.
  try:
    sep_arg = sys.argv[3]
    sep = possible_separators[sep_arg]
  except:
#    If no separator is specified, fall back to the Impala default.
```

```
    sep = "\x01"

# Generate requested number of rows of data.
    for i in xrange(count):

# Column 1 is a sequential integer, starting from 1.
      c1 = str(i+1)

# Column 2 is a random integer, from 0 to the specified upper bound.
# 10% of the time, we substitute a NULL value instead of a number.
      chance = randint(1,10) % 10;
      if chance == 0:
        c2 = r"\N"
      else:
        c2 = str(randint(0,upper))

# Column 3 is another random integer, but formatted with leading
# zeroes to exactly 6 characters.
      c3 = str(randint(0,upper)).zfill(6)

# Column 4 is a random string, from 4-22 characters.
# It is an initial capital letter, followed by 3 sequences of repeating letters.
# 1% of the time, we substitute a NULL value instead of a string.
      chance = randint(1,100) % 100;
      if chance == 0:
        c4 = r"\N"
      else:
        cap = chr(randint(65,90))
        string1 = chr(randint(97,122)) * randint(1,7)
        string2 = chr(randint(97,122)) * randint(1,7)
        string3 = chr(randint(97,122)) * randint(1,7)
        c4 = cap + string1 + string2 + string3

# Column 5 is a random Boolean value.
# It's true 2/3 of the time, false 1/3 of the time.
      bool = randint(0,2)
      if bool == 0:
        c5 = "false"
      else:
        c5 = "true"

# We figure out a random city and state to use for a location field.
      (city,state) = random_city()
      c6 = city
      c7 = state

# Concatenate all the fields and print.
      row = (c1 + sep + c2 + sep + c3 + sep + c4 +
        sep + c5 + sep + c6 + sep + c7)
      print row
```

Impala is flexible in terms of the sequence of operations. You can prepare the data first and even bring it into HDFS, and then construct a database table that matches the structure of the data. Or you can use the traditional sequence of creating the table first and then preparing the data based on the table schema. For this exercise, we'll prepare the data on the local filesystem, then set up the database table in Impala, and then move the data into the expected location in HDFS.

First we run the script to produce the random data. On my Linux server, this takes an hour or more. (This is a good illustration of why it's so attractive to parallelize operations involving so much data.)

```
$ python multicols.py 1000000000 99999 comma >billion_rows.csv
```

Within the impala-shell interpreter, we create a table, which will contain a billion rows after the data files go into HDFS. The attributes of the table (file format, and separator character for text format) match what we used in the raw data files.

```
$ impala-shell -i localhost
[localhost:21000] > create database oreilly;
[localhost:21000] > use oreilly;
[localhost:21000] > create table sample_data
                  > (id bigint, val int, zerofill string, name string,
                  > assertion boolean, city string, state string)
                  > row format delimited fields terminated by ",";
[localhost:21000] > desc sample_data;
+-----------+---------+---------+
| name      | type    | comment |
+-----------+---------+---------+
| id        | bigint  |         |
| val       | int     |         |
| zerofill  | string  |         |
| name      | string  |         |
| assertion | boolean |         |
| city      | string  |         |
| state     | string  |         |
+-----------+---------+---------+
```

Now we need to get the data into the right location in HDFS. To figure out where the data should go, we use the **DESCRIBE FORMATTED** statement:

```
[localhost:21000] > describe formatted sample_data;
...
| # Detailed Table Information | NULL
| Database:                    | oreilly
| Owner:                       | jrussell
| CreateTime:                  | Fri Jul 18 16:25:06 PDT 2014
| LastAccessTime:              | UNKNOWN
| Protect Mode:                | None
| Retention:                   | 0
| Location:                    | hdfs://a1730.abcde.example.com:8020 ❶
|                              | /user/impala/warehouse/oreilly.db/
```

```
|                          | sample_data
| Table Type:              | MANAGED_TABLE
...
```

❶ The Location: attribute represents the HDFS path to the table data. When using
it with Hadoop commands, you can include the hdfs://*host:port* prefix or
leave it out and specify it as a /user/*whoever*/... path.

Armed with this knowledge, we can run Linux utilities (or various kinds of Hadoop
jobs) that deposit data in the appropriate HDFS directory. In this example, we do that
from inside impala-shell using the ! command, which invokes an arbitrary Linux
command.

```
[localhost:21000] > !hdfs dfs -put billion_rows.csv
                  > '/user/impala/warehouse/oreilly.db/sample_data';
```

Impala needs a reminder, in the form of a **REFRESH** statement, whenever data files
are added or changed outside of Impala SQL statements such as **CREATE TABLE AS
SELECT** or **INSERT**. At that point, we can query the table and see that the billion rows
have arrived:

```
[localhost:21000] > refresh sample_data;
[localhost:21000] > select count(*) from sample_data;
+------------+
| count(*)   |
+------------+
| 1000000000 |
+------------+
Returned 1 row(s) in 45.31s
```

Now we've got a billion rows to play with, using all the familiar SQL techniques. Let's
try some simple queries that we know will produce small result sets:

```
[localhost:21000] > select max(name) from sample_data;
+------------------------+
| max(name)              |
+------------------------+
| Zzzzzzzzzzzzzzzzzzzzzz |
+------------------------+
Returned 1 row(s) in 50.73s
[localhost:21000] > select min(name) as first_in_alpha_order, assertion
                  > from sample_data group by assertion;
+----------------------+-----------+
| first_in_alpha_order | assertion |
+----------------------+-----------+
| Aaaa                 | true      |
| Aaaa                 | false     |
+----------------------+-----------+
Returned 2 row(s) in 37.35s
[localhost:21000] > select avg(val), min(name), max(name) from sample_data
                  > where name between 'A' and 'D';
```

```
+---------------------+------------+---------------------------+
| avg(val)            | min(name)  | max(name)                 |
+---------------------+------------+---------------------------+
| 49992.47281834851   | Aaaa       | Czzzzzzzzzzzzzzzzzzzzzz    |
+---------------------+------------+---------------------------+
Returned 1 row(s) in 12.77s
[localhost:21000] > select count(name) as num_names, assertion
                  > from sample_data group by assertion;
+-----------+-----------+
| num_names | assertion |
+-----------+-----------+
| 660023128 | true      |
| 329974394 | false     |
+-----------+-----------+
Returned 2 row(s) in 45.61s
```

What's behind the scenes with these billion rows? We started with one big CSV file and we put it straight into the Hadoop filesystem. The **SHOW TABLE STATS** statement displays the physical characteristics of the table:

```
[localhost:21000] > show table stats sample_data;
+-------+--------+---------+--------------+--------+
| #Rows | #Files | Size    | Bytes Cached | Format |
+-------+--------+---------+--------------+--------+
| -1    | 1      | 56.72GB | NOT CACHED   | TEXT   | ❶
+-------+--------+---------+--------------+--------+
Returned 1 row(s) in 0.01s
```

❶   That single big file is still there in HDFS, all 56.72 gigabytes.

The whole big file is being read every time we do a query, which explains why the queries all take several seconds or more.

At this point, let your inquisitive hacker imagination run free. If there is some way to reduce the data size by several gigabytes, would that translate into seconds shaved off each of these queries? Yes, it would. How about if we could arrange the data so it didn't have to be entirely read for each query? Yes, that would speed up the queries proportionally: read 1/10th as much data, take roughly 1/10th as much time as the original query.

How a Table Works When It's One Big File

Are we losing out on parallelism by having just one file? Not really, because it's so big:

- HDFS internally divides the data up into blocks, 128 MB each by default.

- Each block is replicated to some number of hosts in our cluster; by default 3.

- For each query, each 128 MB block is processed by one of our 4 nodes. Which node processes a given block? That's not entirely predictable, but anyway it's one of the 3 nodes that can read the block off their local disk, rather than asking for it to be sent across the network from a node that does have it. So all 4 of our nodes are kept busy by these queries, and the queries can finish in approximately 1/4 of the time it would take if we did them on a single machine.

Normalizing the Original Data

How are we going to shrink the data? First, let's do a bit of normalization. The CITY and STATE fields only have 289 values total, representing the largest cities in the USA. We could move repeated strings such as "California" and "Mississippi" out of the data file and replace them with small integers.

```
[localhost:21000] > select avg(length(city)) + avg(length(state))
                  > from sample_data;
+---------------------------------------+
| avg(length(city)) + avg(length(state)) |
+---------------------------------------+
| 17.190299006                          | ❶
+---------------------------------------+
Returned 1 row(s) in 15.18s
[localhost:21000] > quit;
```

❶ The average combined length of the CITY and STATE fields is about 17 characters.

We'll replace those with a single number, between 1 and 3 digits. So we could expect to save roughly 15–16 gigabytes of disk space, by replacing 18 characters (CITY and STATE plus comma delimiter) with 2–3 digit numbers.

After we get the data into Impala, we can use SQL skills to slice and dice it in all sorts of ways. Let's set up a tiny lookup table with all the city and state data, and then make a new table with the original data in normalized form. Before transforming the data, we'll use a view to double-check the correctness of the join query that pulls out the normalized values.

Recall that we started with a simple list of `CITY,STATE` values in `usa_cities.lst`. To use this data as a lookup table, we need a file with numeric IDs. That's easy to prepare with basic Unix commands: just take the output of `cat -n`, trim off leading spaces, and turn the tab after the line number into our separator character (comma).

```
$ cat -n usa_cities.lst | sed -e 's/\t/,/' | sed -e 's/^ *//' | tee usa_cities.csv
```

Now we pick up back in the `impala-shell` interpreter, inside the `oreilly` database where we're running these experiments. Again, we load the data file into the right HDFS directory, finding the location with **DESCRIBE FORMATTED** and running the `hdfs` command from inside `impala-shell`:

```
$ impala-shell -i localhost -d oreilly
[localhost:21000] > describe formatted usa_cities;
...
| Location: | hdfs://a1730.abcde.example.com:8020/user/impala/warehouse
|           | /oreilly.db/usa_cities
...
[localhost:21000] > !hdfs dfs -put usa_cities.csv
                  > '/user/impala/warehouse/oreilly.db/usa_cities';
[localhost:21000] > refresh usa_cities;
[localhost:21000] > select count(*) from usa_cities;
+----------+
| count(*) |
+----------+
| 289      |
+----------+
[localhost:21000] > show table stats usa_cities;
+-------+--------+--------+---------------+--------+
| #Rows | #Files | Size   | Bytes Cached  | Format |
+-------+--------+--------+---------------+--------+
| -1    | 1      | 6.44KB | NOT CACHED    | TEXT   |
+-------+--------+--------+---------------+--------+
Returned 1 row(s) in 0.01s
[localhost:21000] > select * from usa_cities limit 5;
+----+--------------+--------------+
| id | city         | state        |
+----+--------------+--------------+
| 1  | New York     | New York     |
| 2  | Los Angeles  | California   |
| 3  | Chicago      | Illinois     |
| 4  | Houston      | Texas        |
| 5  | Philadelphia | Pennsylvania |
+----+--------------+--------------+
```

Before doing any resource-intensive operation like reorganizing the original 56 GB table, I always double-check the logic first using a view, which helps to avoid typing long queries over and over. Let's make sure that the `CITY` and `STATE` data from the original table match up with the values from the new lookup table:

```
[localhost:21000] > create view normalized_view as
               > select one.id, one.val, one.zerofill, one.name,
               >   one.assertion, two.id as location_id
               > from sample_data one join usa_cities two ❶
               > on (one.city = two.city and one.state = two.state);

[localhost:21000] > select one.id, one.location_id,
               >   two.id, two.city, two.state ❷
               > from normalized_view one join usa_cities two
               > on (one.location_id = two.id)
               > limit 5;
+----------+-------------+-----+----------+------------+
| id       | location_id | id  | city     | state      |
+----------+-------------+-----+----------+------------+
| 15840253 | 216         | 216 | Denton   | Texas      |
| 15840254 | 110         | 110 | Fontana  | California |
| 15840255 | 250         | 250 | Gresham  | Oregon     |
| 15840256 | 200         | 200 | Waco     | Texas      |
| 15840257 | 165         | 165 | Escondido| California |
+----------+-------------+-----+----------+------------+
Returned 5 row(s) in 0.42s

[localhost:21000] > select id, city, state from sample_data ❸
               > where id in (15840253, 15840254, 15840255, 15840256, 15840257);
+----------+-----------+------------+
| id       | city      | state      |
+----------+-----------+------------+
| 15840253 | Denton    | Texas      |
| 15840254 | Fontana   | California |
| 15840255 | Gresham   | Oregon     |
| 15840256 | Waco      | Texas      |
| 15840257 | Escondido | California |
+----------+-----------+------------+
Returned 5 row(s) in 5.27s
```

❶ The view gets some columns from the original SAMPLE_DATA table, but retrieves CITY and STATE from the small USA_CITIES lookup table.

❷ The join query pulls CITY and STATE from the small lookup table by way of the view.

❸ The final query confirms that the results are the same when CITY and STATE come from the original SAMPLE_DATA table.

Now we're satisfied that the join query in the view pulls out the correct combination of CITY, STATE, and ID values from the lookup table. So let's create a version of our billion-row table that matches the layout of the view, with the CITY and STATE columns replaced by a single numeric LOCATION_ID:

```
[localhost:21000] > create table normalized_text
                  > row format delimited fields terminated by ","
                  > as select * from normalized_view;
+---------------------------+
| summary                   |
+---------------------------+
| Inserted 1000000000 row(s) |
+---------------------------+
Returned 1 row(s) in 422.06s

[localhost:21000] > select * from normalized_text limit 5;
+-----------+-------+----------+-------------------+-----------+-------------+
| id        | val   | zerofill | name              | assertion | location_id |
+-----------+-------+----------+-------------------+-----------+-------------+
| 921623839 | 95546 | 001301   | Pwwwwwbbe         | false     | 217         |
| 921623840 | 38224 | 018053   | Cllddddddddll     | true      | 127         |
| 921623841 | 73153 | 032797   | Csssijjjjjj       | true      | 124         |
| 921623842 | 35567 | 094193   | Uhhhhhrrrrrrvvv   | false     | 115         |
| 921623843 | 4694  | 051840   | Uccccqqqqqbbbbbb  | true      | 138         |
+-----------+-------+----------+-------------------+-----------+-------------+

[localhost:21000] > show table stats normalized_text;
+-------+--------+---------+--------------+--------+
| #Rows | #Files | Size    | Bytes Cached | Format |
+-------+--------+---------+--------------+--------+
| -1    | 4      | 42.22GB | NOT CACHED   | TEXT   | ❶
+-------+--------+---------+--------------+--------+
```

❶ As predicted, we saved about 14.5 GB in our original table, by creating a lookup table that's less than 7 KB. (From the perspective of the IT group, we've really saved 43.5 GB in total, because each unnecessary data block gets replicated across 3 nodes.)

When we do join queries to display the original city and state names in reports, that is a perfect illustration of the "broadcast" join technique: the lookup table that's only a few KB will be transmitted to each node and cross-referenced against the data from the big table as that larger data set is read from local disk storage.

Q&A

How come when we asked for 5 rows with the `LIMIT 5` clause, we didn't always get the first 5 rows from the table? Some of those queries returned rows with IDs in the range of 15 million or even 921 million.

Remember that as the experiment progressed, the new tables we created had progressively more and more data files: first 4, then 64. Each of our 4 nodes was working on a subset of data, and whichever node came up with its 5 rows first, those are the rows we saw. Even when there was just a single 56 GB file, our 4 nodes were working in parallel on the individual 128 MB data blocks carved out of the original file, and the arbitrary rows we asked for could come back from any of those blocks.

Whenever you expect rows to be returned in a particular order, include an `ORDER BY` clause in the outermost block of a query, or in the query that references the view. The SQL standard does not guarantee sorted results from an `ORDER BY` in a subquery or a view definition.

Converting to Parquet Format

We've just saved several gigabytes of disk space and earned the gratitude of the IT department. Shall we stop there? No, we're on a roll now!

When you read the official Impala documentation, you'll see guidelines saying to use the Parquet file format for all your sizeable tables. This file format uses some clever tricks to shrink the overall size of the data and reduce I/O during queries. Let's give that a try:

```
[localhost:21000] > create table normalized_parquet stored as parquet ❶
                  > as select * from normalized_text;
+---------------------------+
| summary                   |
+---------------------------+
| Inserted 1000000000 row(s) |
+---------------------------+
Returned 1 row(s) in 183.63s
[localhost:21000] > select count(*) from normalized_parquet;
+------------+
| count(*)   |
+------------+
| 1000000000 |
+------------+
Returned 1 row(s) in 2.63s
[localhost:21000] > show table stats normalized_parquet;
+-------+--------+---------+--------------+---------+
| #Rows | #Files | Size    | Bytes Cached | Format  |
+-------+--------+---------+--------------+---------+
```

```
| -1    | 64     | 23.34GB | NOT CACHED   | PARQUET | ❷
+-------+--------+---------+--------------+---------+
Returned 1 row(s) in 0.01s
```

❶ As you gain more experience with Impala queries and performance tuning, you will start to get a warm, fuzzy feeling when you see the STORED AS PARQUET clause in **CREATE TABLE** statements.

❷ Wow, we just reduced the size of the table again—by almost 20 more gigabytes this time. (Again, the 3x replication factor means we saved another 60 GB in total across the cluster).

The ultimate goal is for queries to be faster, so let's see how the various tables we constructed perform with the same queries. We'll run identical queries on the original 56 GB text table, the 42 GB normalized text table, and finally the 23 GB normalized Parquet table, expecting each to be faster than the preceding one:

```
[localhost:21000] > select max(name) from sample_data; ❶
+-----------------------+
| max(name)             |
+-----------------------+
| Zzzzzzzzzzzzzzzzzzzzz |
+-----------------------+
Returned 1 row(s) in 50.73s ❶

[localhost:21000] > select max(name) from normalized_text; ❷
+-----------------------+
| max(name)             |
+-----------------------+
| Zzzzzzzzzzzzzzzzzzzzz |
+-----------------------+
Returned 1 row(s) in 24.15s ❷

[localhost:21000] > select max(name) from normalized_parquet; ❸
+-----------------------+
| max(name)             |
+-----------------------+
| Zzzzzzzzzzzzzzzzzzzzz |
+-----------------------+
Returned 1 row(s) in 20.19s ❸

[localhost:21000] > select avg(val), min(name), max(name)
                  > from sample_data ❶
                  > where name between 'A' and 'D';
+------------------+-----------+-----------------------+
| avg(val)         | min(name) | max(name)             |
+------------------+-----------+-----------------------+
| 49992.47281834851 | Aaaa     | Czzzzzzzzzzzzzzzzzzzz |
+------------------+-----------+-----------------------+
Returned 1 row(s) in 26.36s ❶
```

```
[localhost:21000] > select avg(val), min(name), max(name) from normalized_text ❷
                  > where name between 'A' and 'D';
+-------------------+-----------+------------------------+
| avg(val)          | min(name) | max(name)              |
+-------------------+-----------+------------------------+
| 49992.47281834851 | Aaaa      | Czzzzzzzzzzzzzzzzzzzzz |
+-------------------+-----------+------------------------+
Returned 1 row(s) in 21.17s ❷

[localhost:21000] > select avg(val), min(name), max(name)
                  > from normalized_parquet ❸
                  > where name between 'A' and 'D';
+-------------------+-----------+------------------------+
| avg(val)          | min(name) | max(name)              |
+-------------------+-----------+------------------------+
| 49992.47281834851 | Aaaa      | Czzzzzzzzzzzzzzzzzzzzz |
+-------------------+-----------+------------------------+
Returned 1 row(s) in 12.11s ❸
```

❶ The SAMPLE_DATA is the biggest table, in text format with redundant string data. The queries for this table are the slowest.

❷ The NORMALIZED_TEXT table is somewhat smaller, still in text format. The queries for this table are somewhat faster because of its smaller size, resulting in less I/O.

❸ The NORMALIZED_PARQUET table is the smallest. The queries for this table are the fastest, because the overall data is smaller still, and Parquet reduces I/O even more by reading only the columns needed by the query.

Fun Fact

As I ran and reran these queries in my test environment, the times jumped up and down a bit, because sometimes the Linux servers had cached some of the data after reading it the first time. There again, having the data in the most compact format possible increases the chance that the data will still be cached later, instead of being evicted by reading data that's bulkier than necessary.

As a final experiment with file formats, let's see what happens if we convert the original 56 GB table directly to Parquet without the normalization step. Because we are not eliminating the redundant string data, we can predict that the overall size will be somewhere between the original 56 GB and the 23.34 GB of the NORMALIZED_PARQUET table:

```
localhost:21000] > create table denormalized_parquet stored as parquet as
                  > select * from sample_data;
+----------------------------+
| summary                    |
+----------------------------+
| Inserted 1000000000 row(s) |
```

```
+----------------------------+
Returned 1 row(s) in 225.69s
[localhost:21000] > show table stats denormalized_parquet;
+-------+--------+---------+--------------+---------+
| #Rows | #Files | Size    | Bytes Cached | Format  |
+-------+--------+---------+--------------+---------+
| -1    | 64     | 24.04GB | NOT CACHED   | PARQUET | ❶
+-------+--------+---------+--------------+---------+
Returned 1 row(s) in 0.01s
```

❶   The NORMALIZED_PARQUET table was 23.34 GB, while the DENORMALIZED_PARQUET
      table is only a little bigger at 24.04 GB.

Why isn't there a bigger size difference like there was in text format? When the data was converted to Parquet, it was compacted (encoded) in multiple ways before the final compression step. One trick Parquet uses is to take columns with up to 16K of different values, and internally de-duplicate them, substituting numeric indexes instead of repeated strings. (That technique is known as *dictionary encoding*.) In a sense, Parquet did the same kind of normalization in the original data file, rather than making a separate lookup table. Ideally, you would still normalize such columns and use join queries to look up the original values, but either way, with minimal effort you can get substantial space savings.

Making a Partitioned Table

At this point, the Parquet file format is doing a lot of the heavy lifting to reduce the time for each query by reducing the overall I/O to read the data. If a column is not referenced in the query, Parquet lets the query avoid reading that column entirely, as opposed to text format. For example, in the SAMPLE_DATA and NORMALIZED_TEXT tables we've been using, each query reads 6 GB of data for the ZEROFILL column whether or not that column is used at all. And the compressed and encoded form of the column values means much less data is read even for columns that are needed.

Partitioning the table lets us use our domain knowledge of the data and corresponding queries to reduce the I/O even further. If you have not already read the guidelines for partitioned tables in "Working with Partitioned Tables" on page 39, familiarize yourself with those tips before tackling any real-world projects with partitioning.

In this thought experiment, let's decide that our most common queries will target a subset of users based on the first letter of their names. All else being equal, we could analyze the data for the A users, D users, or X users in about 1/26th of the time it would take to process all users together. In real life, you commonly partition on date-related fields so that you can analyze a certain time period, or on location-related fields so that you can analyze different geographic regions.

Again, because we are going to reorganize several gigabytes of data, let's first make a view that matches the columns of our partitioned table, with a new INITIAL column that represents the first letter of the name:

```
[localhost:21000] > desc normalized_parquet;
+-------------+----------+---------+
| name        | type     | comment |
+-------------+----------+---------+
| id          | bigint   |         |
| val         | int      |         |
| zerofill    | string   |         |
| name        | string   |         |
| assertion   | boolean  |         |
| location_id | smallint |         |
+-------------+----------+---------+
Returned 6 row(s) in 0.01s

[localhost:21000] > create view partitioned_normalized_view as
                  > select id, val, zerofill, name, assertion, location_id,
                  > substr(name,1,1) as initial ❶
                  > from normalized_parquet;
Returned 0 row(s) in 2.89s

[localhost:21000] > select id, name, initial
                  > from partitioned_normalized_view limit 5;
+-----------+----------------------+---------+
| id        | name                 | initial |
+-----------+----------------------+---------+
| 663027574 | Ckkvvvvvvvmmmmmm     | C       |
| 663027575 | Fkkkkkkkwwwwwwyyyyy  | F       |
| 663027576 | Orrrrrrrfmmmmm       | O       |
| 663027577 | Peeevvvvvvvvvv       | P       |
| 663027578 | Dmmmmhhhs            | D       |
+-----------+----------------------+---------+
Returned 5 row(s) in 4.65s
```

❶ For partition key columns, we would normally use the verbatim column values from the original data where appropriate. In this case, however, we make a new partition key column by running a function on the original values.

After we're satisfied that the new INITIAL column has the right values, we create a partitioned table using the PARTITIONED BY clause, and copy the data into it from the unpartitioned table:

```
[localhost:21000] > create table partitioned_normalized_parquet
                  > (id bigint, val int, zerofill string, name string,
                  > assertion boolean, location_id smallint)
                  > partitioned by (initial string) stored as parquet; ❶
Returned 0 row(s) in 1.81s
[localhost:21000] > insert into partitioned_normalized_parquet partition(initial)
```

```
                      > select * from partitioned_normalized_view; ❷
      Inserted 1000000000 rows in 619.28s
```

❶   The INITIAL column is referenced by the PARTITIONED BY clause, not in the
     regular column list.

❷   The **SELECT** * portion of the **INSERT** statement requires that the regular columns
     come first, then any partition key columns last. This is another reason we use a
     view—to specify the columns in the most convenient order for the **INSERT**
     statement.

Now let's examine how the data is broken down within the partitioned table:

```
[localhost:21000] > show table stats partitioned_normalized_parquet;
+---------+-------+--------+----------+--------------+---------+
| initial | #Rows | #Files | Size     | Bytes Cached | Format  |
+---------+-------+--------+----------+--------------+---------+
| A       | -1    | 3      | 871.79MB | NOT CACHED   | PARQUET | ❶
| B       | -1    | 3      | 871.72MB | NOT CACHED   | PARQUET |
| C       | -1    | 3      | 871.40MB | NOT CACHED   | PARQUET |
| D       | -1    | 3      | 871.64MB | NOT CACHED   | PARQUET |
| E       | -1    | 3      | 871.54MB | NOT CACHED   | PARQUET |
| F       | -1    | 3      | 871.11MB | NOT CACHED   | PARQUET |
| G       | -1    | 3      | 871.29MB | NOT CACHED   | PARQUET |
| H       | -1    | 3      | 871.42MB | NOT CACHED   | PARQUET |
| K       | -1    | 3      | 871.42MB | NOT CACHED   | PARQUET |
| L       | -1    | 3      | 871.31MB | NOT CACHED   | PARQUET |
| M       | -1    | 3      | 871.38MB | NOT CACHED   | PARQUET |
| N       | -1    | 3      | 871.25MB | NOT CACHED   | PARQUET |
| O       | -1    | 3      | 871.14MB | NOT CACHED   | PARQUET |
| P       | -1    | 3      | 871.44MB | NOT CACHED   | PARQUET |
| Q       | -1    | 3      | 871.55MB | NOT CACHED   | PARQUET |
| R       | -1    | 3      | 871.30MB | NOT CACHED   | PARQUET |
| S       | -1    | 3      | 871.50MB | NOT CACHED   | PARQUET |
| T       | -1    | 3      | 871.65MB | NOT CACHED   | PARQUET |
| Y       | -1    | 3      | 871.57MB | NOT CACHED   | PARQUET |
| Z       | -1    | 3      | 871.54MB | NOT CACHED   | PARQUET |
| NULL    | -1    | 1      | 147.30MB | NOT CACHED   | PARQUET | ❷
| I       | -1    | 3      | 871.44MB | NOT CACHED   | PARQUET |
| J       | -1    | 3      | 871.32MB | NOT CACHED   | PARQUET |
| U       | -1    | 3      | 871.36MB | NOT CACHED   | PARQUET |
| V       | -1    | 3      | 871.39MB | NOT CACHED   | PARQUET |
| W       | -1    | 3      | 871.79MB | NOT CACHED   | PARQUET |
| X       | -1    | 3      | 871.95MB | NOT CACHED   | PARQUET |
| Total   | -1    | 79     | 22.27GB  | 0B           |         |
+---------+-------+--------+----------+--------------+---------+
Returned 28 row(s) in 0.04s
```

❶   Each partition has less than 1 GB of data.

❷ The NULL partition is a reminder that our original data-generating script included some NULL values in the NAME column, which carried over to the INITIAL column we're using as the partition key. This is something to check for during validation and cleansing operations, to make sure that some rows do not become "orphaned" by having null partition keys that never get matched by the WHERE clauses in your queries.

Now when we run queries that target just one or a few partitions, the query reads 3 files totalling less than 1 GB for each partition that is processed.

Partitioned tables are best for queries that access a small proportion of the total partitions.

```
[localhost:21000] > select avg(val), min(name), max(name)
                  > from normalized_parquet where substr(name,1,1) = 'Q';
+-------------------+-----------+------------------------+
| avg(val)          | min(name) | max(name)              |
+-------------------+-----------+------------------------+
| 50001.94660836487 | Qaaa      | Qzzzzzzzzzzzzzzzzzzzzz |
+-------------------+-----------+------------------------+
Returned 1 row(s) in 5.74s ❶

[localhost:21000] > select avg(val), min(name), max(name)
                  > from partitioned_normalized_parquet where initial = 'Q';
+-------------------+-----------+------------------------+
| avg(val)          | min(name) | max(name)              |
+-------------------+-----------+------------------------+
| 50001.94660836487 | Qaaa      | Qzzzzzzzzzzzzzzzzzzzzz |
+-------------------+-----------+------------------------+
Returned 1 row(s) in 4.75s ❷

[localhost:21000] > select avg(val), min(name), max(name)
                  > from normalized_parquet
                  > where substr(name,1,1) between 'A' and 'C';
+-------------------+-----------+------------------------+
| avg(val)          | min(name) | max(name)              |
+-------------------+-----------+------------------------+
| 49994.3356542968  | Aaaa      | Czzzzzzzzzzzzzzzzzzzzz |
+-------------------+-----------+------------------------+
Returned 1 row(s) in 11.65s ❸

[localhost:21000] > select avg(val), min(name), max(name)
                  > from partitioned_normalized_parquet
                  > where initial between 'A' and 'C';
+-------------------+-----------+------------------------+
| avg(val)          | min(name) | max(name)              |
+-------------------+-----------+------------------------+
| 49992.47281834851 | Aaaa      | Czzzzzzzzzzzzzzzzzzzzz |
+-------------------+-----------+------------------------+
Returned 1 row(s) in 8.91s ❹
```

❶ This query scans the whole table and analyzes the rows where the `NAME` column starts with a particular letter.

❷ An equivalent query that touches one partition in the partitioned table is a little bit faster. It's not 26 times faster though, due to the arithmetic having to do with block sizes, number of files, number of hosts in the cluster, and number of cores per host. Some of the resources across the cluster might sit idle during a particular query because there is just not enough data to require getting all hosts and cores involved. Here we are with a billion-row table, and still there is not enough data to really demonstrate all the potential performance benefits. On the other hand, the fact that there is still idle capacity is good news for scalability: the cluster could run many other concurrent queries without maxing out the available CPUs or storage devices.

❸ This query against the unpartitioned table reads all the data and analyzes all rows where the `NAME` field starts with one of three different letters.

❹ An equivalent query that touches three partitions in the partitioned table is again a little bit faster. The speedup is more noticeable as the volume of data in the table increases, and as the number of partitions increases.

Let's see what happens with a query that scans the entire table:

```
[localhost:21000] > select avg(val), min(name), max(name)
                  > from partitioned_normalized_parquet;
+-------------------+-----------+------------------------+
| avg(val)          | min(name) | max(name)              |
+-------------------+-----------+------------------------+
| 49998.04368627915 | Aaaa      | Zzzzzzzzzzzzzzzzzzzzz  |
+-------------------+-----------+------------------------+
Returned 1 row(s) in 69.29s ❶
[localhost:21000] > select avg(val), min(name), max(name)
                  > from normalized_parquet;
+-------------------+-----------+------------------------+
| avg(val)          | min(name) | max(name)              |
+-------------------+-----------+------------------------+
| 49998.04368627915 | Aaaa      | Zzzzzzzzzzzzzzzzzzzzz  |
+-------------------+-----------+------------------------+
Returned 1 row(s) in 68.26s ❶
```

❶ For a query that does a full-table scan, the partitioned table is actually a little slower than the unpartitioned one. Having to process all the different data files from the partition directories adds a bit of overhead. That's why it's important to partition on the columns that you actually use for filtering in your most important and most frequent queries.

Next Steps

At this point, we've done a reasonable job of optimizing single-table queries for our billion rows of sample data. From here, there are two other kinds of scenarios to explore:

- If you know that certain tables or partitions will be queried intensively, you can enable HDFS caching to ensure they are held in memory. To use this feature in production and to understand the performance and scalability aspects typically requires coordinating with your system administrator (see "Helping to Plan for Performance (Stats, HDFS Caching)" on page 44).

- Going farther with normalization or cross-referencing different kinds of data sets means doing a lot of join queries. Join queries have their own set of performance considerations, as shown in the next section, "Deep Dive: Joins and the Role of Statistics".

Deep Dive: Joins and the Role of Statistics

When dealing with large and ever-growing tables, Impala can better optimize complex queries (especially join queries) the more it knows about the characteristics of the data, both at the table level and the column level. The Impala SQL statement to collect such information is **COMPUTE STATS**. Run this statement after loading substantial new data into a table.

Creating a Million-Row Table to Join With

First, we create a table with the same structure as our original billion-row table ("Tutorial: The Journey of a Billion Rows" on page 51). We will take a sample of a million rows from our billion rows of data, then do joins between the big table and the small table:

```
[localhost:21000] > create table stats_demo like sample_data;
[localhost:21000] > show table stats stats_demo;
+-------+--------+------+--------------+--------+
| #Rows | #Files | Size | Bytes Cached | Format |
+-------+--------+------+--------------+--------+
| -1    | 0      | 0B   | NOT CACHED   | TEXT   |
+-------+--------+------+--------------+--------+
[localhost:21000] > show column stats stats_demo;
+-----------+---------+-----------------+--------+----------+----------+
| Column    | Type    | #Distinct Values | #Nulls | Max Size | Avg Size |
+-----------+---------+-----------------+--------+----------+----------+
| id        | BIGINT  | -1              | -1     | 8        | 8        |  ❶
| val       | INT     | -1              | -1     | 4        | 4        |
| zerofill  | STRING  | -1              | -1     | -1       | -1       |  ❷
| name      | STRING  | -1              | -1     | -1       | -1       |
| assertion | BOOLEAN | -1              | -1     | 1        | 1        |
```

```
| city     | STRING  | -1                |  -1    |  -1     |  -1      |
| state    | STRING  | -1                |  -1    |  -1     |  -1      |
+----------+---------+-------------------+--------+---------+---------+
```

❶ Initially, Impala knows basic physical properties based on the data files and the schema, such as the total data size and the sizes of numeric columns, which never vary in length.

❷ The `-1` numbers indicate properties where Impala does not know the values. The unknown values are most prominent for STRING columns, with values that vary in size.

Loading Data and Computing Stats

In the following example, we load a million rows into the table and collect statistics for the data. To help Impala choose a good query plan for a join involving this table, it's important to know the characteristics of the various columns.

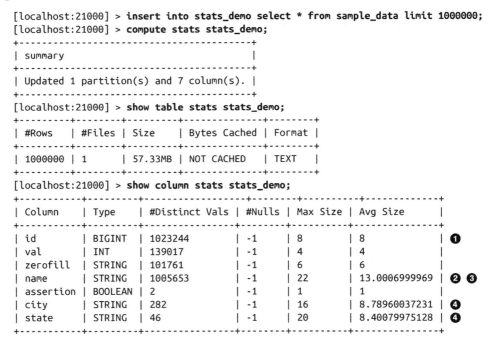

```
[localhost:21000] > insert into stats_demo select * from sample_data limit 1000000;
[localhost:21000] > compute stats stats_demo;
+------------------------------------------+
| summary                                  |
+------------------------------------------+
| Updated 1 partition(s) and 7 column(s).  |
+------------------------------------------+
[localhost:21000] > show table stats stats_demo;
+---------+--------+---------+--------------+--------+
| #Rows   | #Files | Size    | Bytes Cached | Format |
+---------+--------+---------+--------------+--------+
| 1000000 | 1      | 57.33MB | NOT CACHED   | TEXT   |
+---------+--------+---------+--------------+--------+
[localhost:21000] > show column stats stats_demo;
+----------+---------+----------------+--------+----------+---------------+
| Column   | Type    | #Distinct Vals | #Nulls | Max Size | Avg Size      |
+----------+---------+----------------+--------+----------+---------------+
| id       | BIGINT  | 1023244        | -1     | 8        | 8             | ❶
| val      | INT     | 139017         | -1     | 4        | 4             |
| zerofill | STRING  | 101761         | -1     | 6        | 6             |
| name     | STRING  | 1005653        | -1     | 22       | 13.0006999969 | ❷ ❸
| assertion| BOOLEAN | 2              | -1     | 1        | 1             |
| city     | STRING  | 282            | -1     | 16       | 8.78960037231 | ❹
| state    | STRING  | 46             | -1     | 20       | 8.40079975128 | ❹
+----------+---------+----------------+--------+----------+---------------+
```

❶ Currently, the number of nulls is not counted because the planner doesn't use this information.

❷ The ID and NAME columns contain essentially unique values. The NAME field tends to be longer than the CITY and STATE fields.

❸ The number of distinct values is estimated rather than counted precisely, because the planner only needs a rough estimate to judge whether one approach is faster than another. For example, the estimate for the NAME column is slightly higher than the actual number of rows in the table. Impala automatically adjusts the estimate downward in such a case.

❹ The CITY and STATE columns have very few distinct values.

Reviewing the EXPLAIN Plan

In a join query involving tables of different sizes, Impala automatically determines the following:

- Which tables to read from local storage devices on the data nodes.
- Which tables are small enough to send in their entirety to each node.
- Which tables to split up and transmit smaller pieces to different nodes.
- The optimal order of these operations, to minimize data transmission and the size of the intermediate result sets from each stage of join processing.

You can see the results by looking at the **EXPLAIN** plan for a query, without the need to actually run it:

```
[localhost:21000] > explain select count(*) from sample_data join stats_demo
                  > using (id) where substr(sample_data.name,1,1) = 'G';
+-------------------------------------------------------------------+
| Explain String                                                    |
+-------------------------------------------------------------------+
| Estimated Per-Host Requirements: Memory=5.75GB VCores=2           |
| WARNING: The following tables are missing relevant table          |
|          and/or column statistics.                                | ❶
| oreilly.sample_data                                               |
|                                                                   |
| 06:AGGREGATE [MERGE FINALIZE]                                     |
| |   output: sum(count(*))                                         |
| |                                                                 |
| 05:EXCHANGE [UNPARTITIONED]                                       |
| |                                                                 |
| 03:AGGREGATE                                                      |
| |   output: count(*)                                              |
| |                                                                 |
| 02:HASH JOIN [INNER JOIN, BROADCAST]                              |
| |   hash predicates: oreilly.stats_demo.id = oreilly.sample_data.id |
| |                                                                 |
| |--04:EXCHANGE [BROADCAST]                                        |
| |  |                                                              |
| |  00:SCAN HDFS [oreilly.sample_data]                             | ❷
| |     partitions=1/1 size=56.72GB                                 |
| |     predicates: substr(sample_data.name, 1, 1) = 'G'           |
```

```
|  |                                                                         |
| 01:SCAN HDFS [oreilly.stats_demo]                                         | ❸
|     partitions=1/1 size=57.33MB                                           |
+---------------------------------------------------------------------------+
```

❶ Wait a second. That warning at the top of the plan output reminds us that although we just ran **COMPUTE STATS** for our new table, we neglected to do it for our oldest (and biggest) table.

❷ When Impala reports that it is going to "scan HDFS" for the SAMPLE_DATA table and then "broadcast" the result, that is an expensive network operation: it sends the results from scanning SAMPLE_DATA and extracting the G names to each node to compare and contrast against the STATS_DEMO table. That's about 1/26th of 56.72 GB (about 2.2 GB) being sent to each of four nodes. It's preferable to see a small amount of data being broadcast. Maybe we can reduce the amount of network I/O.

❸ To understand the flow of the query, you read from bottom to top. (After checking any warnings at the top.) For a join query, you prefer to see the biggest table listed at the bottom, then the smallest, second smallest, third smallest, and so on.

When Impala sees a table with no statistics used in a join query (like SAMPLE_DATA in this case), it treats the table like it is zero-sized, as if it is no problem to send over the network. That is clearly wrong in this case, where SAMPLE_DATA is bigger and has more different values in both the ID and NAME columns referenced in the query.

Let's collect statistics for the big (billion-row) SAMPLE_DATA table, too, and then try again:

```
[localhost:21000] > compute stats sample_data; ❶
+-----------------------------------------+
| summary                                 |
+-----------------------------------------+
| Updated 1 partition(s) and 7 column(s). |
+-----------------------------------------+
[localhost:21000] > show table stats sample_data;
+------------+--------+---------+---------------+--------+
| #Rows      | #Files | Size    | Bytes Cached  | Format |
+------------+--------+---------+---------------+--------+
| 1000000000 | 1      | 56.72GB | NOT CACHED    | TEXT   | ❷
+------------+--------+---------+---------------+--------+
[localhost:21000] > show column stats sample_data;
+-----------+---------+----------------+--------+----------+----------------+
| Column    | Type    | #Distinct Vals | #Nulls | Max Size | Avg Size       |
+-----------+---------+----------------+--------+----------+----------------+
| id        | BIGINT  | 183861280      | 0      | 8        | 8              |
| val       | INT     | 139017         | 0      | 4        | 4              |
| zerofill  | STRING  | 101761         | 0      | 6        | 6              |
| name      | STRING  | 145636240      | 0      | 22       | 13.0002002716  | ❸
| assertion | BOOLEAN | 2              | 0      | 1        | 1              |
```

```
| city      | STRING | 282             | 0       | 16        | 8.78890037536  |
| state     | STRING | 46              | 0       | 20        | 8.40139961242  |
+-----------+--------+-----------------+---------+-----------+----------------+
```

❶ The **COMPUTE STATS** statement is the key to improving the efficiency of join queries. Now we've run it for all tables involved in the join.

❷ The key item of information for the table stats is the number of rows.

❸ In the column stats, Impala estimates the number of distinct values for each column and examines STRING columns to find the maximum and average length.

```
[localhost:21000] > explain select count(*) from sample_data join stats_demo
                  > using (id) where substr(sample_data.name,1,1) = 'G';
+-------------------------------------------------------------------+
| Explain String                                                    |
+-------------------------------------------------------------------+
| Estimated Per-Host Requirements: Memory=3.77GB VCores=2           |
|                                                                   |
| 06:AGGREGATE [MERGE FINALIZE]                                     |
| |   output: sum(count(*))                                         |
| |                                                                 |
| 05:EXCHANGE [UNPARTITIONED]                                       |
| |                                                                 |
| 03:AGGREGATE                                                      |
| |   output: count(*)                                              |
| |                                                                 |
| 02:HASH JOIN [INNER JOIN, BROADCAST]                              |
| |   hash predicates: oreilly.sample_data.id = oreilly.stats_demo.id |
| |                                                                 |
| |--04:EXCHANGE [BROADCAST]                                        |
| |  |                                                              |
| |  01:SCAN HDFS [oreilly.stats_demo]                              |      ❶
| |     partitions=1/1 size=57.33MB                                 |
| |                                                                 |
| 00:SCAN HDFS [oreilly.sample_data]                                |      ❷
|    partitions=1/1 size=56.72GB                                    |
|    predicates: substr(sample_data.name, 1, 1) = 'G'               |      ❸
+-------------------------------------------------------------------+
```

❶ This time, the smaller STATS_DEMO table is broadcast in its entirety to all the four nodes. Instead of sending about 2.2 GB across the network to each node as in the previous query, we're only sending about 57.33 MB, which is the size of the smaller table. We've just improved the efficiency of our query by a factor of about 38, without actually running either the slow or the fast version. That's much better!

❷ The data that's broadcasted is cross-checked against the big SAMPLE_DATA table. Each of our four nodes will read 1/4 of this table from local storage. For join queries, we always want to see the biggest table at the bottom of the plan, meaning that the data from that table is read locally rather than being sent over the network.

❸ We know that most of the 56.72 GB will be ignored and not need to be cross-checked against the other table, because it will not match the predicate that checks for the first letter 'G'. Impala does not yet account for that aspect in the plan numbers. We'll improve on that as we progress to using partitioned tables.

Trying a Real Query

Just for kicks, let's try this query out in real life:

```
[localhost:21000] > select count(*) from sample_data join stats_demo
                   > using (id) where substr(sample_data.name,1,1) = 'G';
+----------+
| count(*) |
+----------+
| 37763    |
+----------+
Returned 1 row(s) in 13.35s
```

By joining a table of a billion rows with a table of a million rows, we checked a million billion possible combinations. The results came back so fast, there was hardly enough time to play one move in Words with Friends™. (All timing numbers in this book are from a small cluster of modest capacity; I expect you to be able to beat them without much trouble.)

Remember that we demonstrated earlier that text tables are bulkier than they need to be, and we could trim things down and speed things up by converting to Parquet, doing some normalization, and introducing partitioning. Let's try again with the more efficient tables we set up using that same data. (We don't expect the count returned by the query to be exactly the same, because we're taking a random sample of a million rows to copy into the new table.)

```
[localhost:21000] > create table stats_demo_parquet
                   >   like partitioned_normalized_parquet; ❶
Returned 0 row(s) in 1.14s

[localhost:21000] > insert into stats_demo_parquet partition (initial)
                   > [shuffle] select * from partitioned_normalized_parquet ❷
                   > limit 1000000;
Inserted 1000000 rows in 39.72s
```

❶ The **CREATE TABLE LIKE** statement preserves the file format of the original table, so we know the new one will use Parquet format also.

❷ We use the [SHUFFLE] hint technique to avoid having each of the four nodes try to allocate 27 GB-sized buffers to write separate data files for all the partition values. The "shuffle" operation takes a little longer, but avoids potential out-of-memory conditions. This is the default Impala uses when a table has no statistics, so strictly speaking, it is only necessary if Impala chooses the wrong execution plan for some reason, such as out-of-date statistics.

Again, we make sure to run the **COMPUTE STATS** statement for all the tables involved in the join query, after loading the data. In earlier examples with tables like PARTITIONED_NORMALIZED_PARQUET, we saw a little under 1 GB of data in each partition. In the smaller table containing a random sample of the data, each partition contains substantially less data.

```
[localhost:21000] > compute stats partitioned_normalized_parquet;
+----------------------------------------+
| summary                                |
+----------------------------------------+
| Updated 26 partition(s) and 6 column(s). |
+----------------------------------------+
Returned 1 row(s) in 54.24s
[localhost:21000] > compute stats stats_demo_parquet;
+----------------------------------------+
| summary                                |
+----------------------------------------+
| Updated 26 partition(s) and 6 column(s). |
+----------------------------------------+
Returned 1 row(s) in 4.86s
[localhost:21000] > show table stats stats_demo_parquet;
+---------+---------+--------+----------+--------------+---------+
| initial | #Rows   | #Files | Size     | Bytes Cached | Format  |
+---------+---------+--------+----------+--------------+---------+
| A       | 89088   | 1      | 2.34MB   | NOT CACHED   | PARQUET |
| B       | 46080   | 1      | 1.31MB   | NOT CACHED   | PARQUET |
| C       | 219136  | 1      | 5.28MB   | NOT CACHED   | PARQUET |
| D       | 63488   | 1      | 1.77MB   | NOT CACHED   | PARQUET |
| E       | 49152   | 1      | 1.39MB   | NOT CACHED   | PARQUET |
| F       | 32768   | 1      | 960.64KB | NOT CACHED   | PARQUET |
| G       | 11264   | 1      | 336.67KB | NOT CACHED   | PARQUET |
| ...     |         |        |          |              |         |
| W       | 16384   | 1      | 484.57KB | NOT CACHED   | PARQUET |
| X       | 51200   | 1      | 1.45MB   | NOT CACHED   | PARQUET |
| NULL    | -1      | 1      | 181.73KB | NOT CACHED   | PARQUET |
| Y       | 82944   | 1      | 2.21MB   | NOT CACHED   | PARQUET |
| Z       | 27648   | 1      | 816.00KB | NOT CACHED   | PARQUET |
| Total   | 1000000 | 27     | 26.99MB  | 0B           |         |
+---------+---------+--------+----------+--------------+---------+
Returned 28 row(s) in 0.02s
```

Now we go through the same exercise as before, running an **EXPLAIN** statement and examining the amount of data expected to be read from disk and transmitted across the network:

```
[localhost:21000] > explain select count(*) from partitioned_normalized_parquet
                  > join stats_demo_parquet using (id)
                  > where
                  > substr(partitioned_normalized_parquet.name,1,1) = 'G'; ❶
+------------------------------------------------------------------------------+
| Explain String                                                               |
+------------------------------------------------------------------------------+
| Estimated Per-Host Requirements: Memory=194.31MB VCores=2                     |
|                                                                              |
| 06:AGGREGATE [MERGE FINALIZE]                                                 |
| |   output: sum(count(*))                                                     |
| |                                                                            |
| 05:EXCHANGE [UNPARTITIONED]                                                   |
| |                                                                            |
| 03:AGGREGATE                                                                  |
| |   output: count(*)                                                          |
| |                                                                            |
| 02:HASH JOIN [INNER JOIN, BROADCAST]                                          |
| |   hash predicates: oreilly.partitioned_normalized_parquet.id =             |
| |     oreilly.stats_demo_parquet.id                                          |
| |                                                                            |
| |--04:EXCHANGE [BROADCAST]                                                    |
| |   |                                                                        |
| |   01:SCAN HDFS [oreilly.stats_demo_parquet]                                 |
| |       partitions=27/27 size=26.99MB                                        | ❷
| |                                                                            |
| 00:SCAN HDFS [oreilly.partitioned_normalized_parquet]                         |
|     partitions=27/27 size=22.27GB                                            | ❸
|     predicates: substr(partitioned_normalized_parquet.name, 1, 1) = 'G'     | ❹
+------------------------------------------------------------------------------+
Returned 21 row(s) in 0.03s
```

Those "scan" figures at the bottom are looking better than with the text tables.

❶ The query does a naive translation of the original query with the SUBSTR() call.

❷ We're going to transmit ("broadcast") 26.99 MB across the network to each node.

❸ We're going to read 22.27 GB from disk. This is the I/O-intensive part of this query, which occurs on the nodes that hold data blocks from the biggest table. Because we usually read these plans bottom to top, this is the first figure to consider in evaluating if the query is executing the way we want it to.

❹ Calling a function in the WHERE clause is not always a smart move, because that function can be called so many times. Now that the first letter is available in a column, maybe it would be more efficient to refer to the INITIAL column.

The following example improves the query for the partitioned table by testing the first letter directly, referencing the INITIAL column instead of calling SUBSTR(). The more we can refer to the partition key columns, the better Impala can ignore all the irrelevant partitions.

```
[localhost:21000] > explain select count(*) from partitioned_normalized_parquet
                  > join stats_demo_parquet using (id)                         ❶
                  > where partitioned_normalized_parquet.initial = 'G';        ❷
+---------------------------------------------------------------------+
| Explain String                                                      |
+---------------------------------------------------------------------+
| Estimated Per-Host Requirements: Memory=106.31MB VCores=2           |
|                                                                     |
| 06:AGGREGATE [MERGE FINALIZE]                                       |
| |   output: sum(count(*))                                           |
| |                                                                   |
| 05:EXCHANGE [UNPARTITIONED]                                         |
| |                                                                   |
| 03:AGGREGATE                                                        |
| |   output: count(*)                                                |
| |                                                                   |
| 02:HASH JOIN [INNER JOIN, BROADCAST]                                |
| |   hash predicates: oreilly.partitioned_normalized_parquet.id =    |
| |     oreilly.stats_demo_parquet.id                                 |
| |                                                                   |
| |--04:EXCHANGE [BROADCAST]                                          |
| |  |                                                                |
| |  01:SCAN HDFS [oreilly.stats_demo_parquet]                        |
| |     partitions=27/27 size=26.99MB                                 |
| |                                                                   |
| 00:SCAN HDFS [oreilly.partitioned_normalized_parquet]               |
|    partitions=1/27 size=871.29MB                                    | ❷
+---------------------------------------------------------------------+
Returned 20 row(s) in 0.02s
```

❶ Our join clause is USING(id) because all the corresponding rows have matching ID values.

❷ By replacing the SUBSTR() call with a reference to the partition key column, we really chopped down how much data has to be read from disk in the first phase: now it's less than 1 GB instead of 22.27 GB.

We happen to know (although Impala doesn't know) that rows with the same ID value will also have the same INITIAL value. Let's add INITIAL to the USING clause and see if that helps.

```
[localhost:21000] > explain select count(*) from partitioned_normalized_parquet
                  > join stats_demo_parquet using (id,initial) ❶
                  > where partitioned_normalized_parquet.initial = 'G';
+---------------------------------------------------------------------+
| Explain String                                                      |
```

```
+----------------------------------------------------------------+
| Estimated Per-Host Requirements: Memory=98.27MB VCores=2       |
|                                                                |
| 06:AGGREGATE [MERGE FINALIZE]                                  |
| |   output: sum(count(*))                                      |
| |                                                              |
| 05:EXCHANGE [UNPARTITIONED]                                    |
| |                                                              |
| 03:AGGREGATE                                                   |
| |   output: count(*)                                           |
| |                                                              |
| 02:HASH JOIN [INNER JOIN, BROADCAST]                           |
| |   hash predicates: oreilly.partitioned_normalized_parquet.id = |
| |       oreilly.stats_demo_parquet.id,                         |
| |       oreilly.partitioned_normalized_parquet.initial =       |
| |       oreilly.stats_demo_parquet.initial                     |
| |                                                              |
| |--04:EXCHANGE [BROADCAST]                                     |
| |  |                                                           |
| |  01:SCAN HDFS [oreilly.stats_demo_parquet]                   |
| |      partitions=1/27 size=336.67KB                           |
| |                                                              |
| 00:SCAN HDFS [oreilly.partitioned_normalized_parquet]         |
|     partitions=1/27 size=871.29MB                              |
+----------------------------------------------------------------+
Returned 20 row(s) in 0.02s
```

❶   Now the USING clause references two columns that must both match in both tables.

❷   Now instead of transmitting 26.99 MB (the entire smaller table) across the network, we're transmitting 336.67 KB, the size of the G partition in the smaller table.

This looks really promising. We've gone from transmitting gigabytes across the network for each query, to under a megabyte. Again, even as we iterated through several variations of the query, we didn't have to actually try them and run the risk of executing a really slow, resource-intensive one.

The Story So Far

Just to recap, we took the following optimization steps, starting from our original bulky text table:

1. Converted the data to Parquet file format.
2. Normalized the data to reduce redundancy.
3. Partitioned the data to quickly locate ranges of values.
4. Computed the stats for both tables involved in the join query.

5. Referenced the partition key columns wherever practical in the query itself, especially in the join and WHERE clauses.

6. Used **EXPLAIN** to get an idea of the efficiency of possible queries as we iterated through several alternatives.

Final Join Query with 1B x 1M Rows

Now let's see how the query performs in real life after going through several iterations of fine-tuning it and checking the **EXPLAIN** plan:

```
[localhost:21000] > select count(*) from partitioned_normalized_parquet
                  > join stats_demo_parquet using (id,initial)
                  > where partitioned_normalized_parquet.initial = 'G';
+----------+
| count(*) |
+----------+
| 11264    |
+----------+
Returned 1 row(s) in 1.87s
```

That's a million billion potential combinations being evaluated in less than 2 seconds, on a 4-node cluster with modest hardware specs. (For example, these nodes have 48 GB of memory each, which is much less than in a typical Impala cluster.)

Anti-Pattern: A Million Little Pieces

One common anti-pattern to avoid is what's known as the "many small files" problem. Hadoop, HDFS, and Impala are all optimized to work with multimegabyte files. Ingesting data that was not originally organized for Hadoop can result in a profusion of tiny data files, leading to suboptimal performance even though the volume of data being read is small. The overhead of distributing a parallel query across a cluster isn't worthwhile if the data is fragmented into a few kilobytes or even a few megabytes per file.

The techniques you want to avoid are:

- Running a sequence of **INSERT ... VALUES** statements, especially with a single item in the VALUES clause. If you need to build up a data file line by line, use a technique outside of Impala such as running Sqoop or Flume, or writing your own data-generation program (possibly running it as a MapReduce job).

- Partitioning down to the most granular level possible, so that the table contains thousands or tens of thousands of partitions, and each partition has only a tiny amount of data. Sometimes, Impala tables do best with one less level of partitioning than you might be used to, such as year and month rather than year, month, and day.

- Inserting into a table with lots of partitions, using a *dynamic* **INSERT ... SELECT** statement. The dynamic form of this statement divides the data among multiple partitions at runtime, based on values in the **SELECT** query. The **INSERT** goes faster if you specify the partition key values as constants and operate on one partition at a time.

Ways to avoid or recover from this kind of problem include:

- If you create a lookup table with a predictable set of hardcoded values, do it with a single VALUES clause:

```
INSERT INTO canada_regions VALUES
  ("Newfoundland and Labrador" ,"NL"),
  ("Prince Edward Island","PE"),
  ("New Brunswick","NB"), ("Nova Scotia","NS"),
  ("Quebec","PQ"), ("Ontario","ON"),
  ("Manitoba","MB"), ("Saskatchewan","SK"), ("Alberta","AB"),
  ("British Columbia","BC"), ("YT","Yukon"),
  ("Northwest Territories","NT"), ("Nunavut","NU");
```

This technique generates a single data file; although it's still tiny in comparison to the 128 MB block size in HDFS, it's more efficient than a dozen separate data files containing one row each!

- If you have a table with an inefficient file layout, coalesce the data by copying the entire contents to a different table with an **INSERT ... SELECT** operation. The output data files will be reorganized based on the number of nodes in your cluster and the number of cores per node.

- When loading into a partitioned table, where practical, insert the data one partition at a time:

```
INSERT INTO sales_data PARTITION (year=2014, month=07)
  SELECT customer, product, amount, purchase_date FROM raw_data
  WHERE year = 2014 AND month = 07;
```

- You can minimize disruption from coalescing data into a new table by pointing all your reporting queries at a view and switching the table that's accessed by the view:

```
CREATE VIEW production_report AS SELECT ... FROM original_table WHERE ...;
INSERT INTO optimized_table SELECT * FROM original_table;
COMPUTE STATS optimized_table;
ALTER VIEW production_report AS SELECT ... FROM optimized_table WHERE ...;
```

This way, all your query-intensive applications can refer to a consistent name, even if you reorganize the data behind the scenes. The new table could use the Parquet file format, partitioning, or more compact data types than the original.

- When inserting into a partitioned table, have accurate table and column statistics on the table holding the original data. Use the **SHOW TABLE STATS** and **SHOW COLUMN**

STATS to check if the stats are present and accurate (particularly the "number of rows" figure in the table statistics). Use the **COMPUTE STATS** statement to collect the statistics if that information is missing or substantially different from the current contents of the source table.

- When doing an insert operation across multiple partitions in a Parquet table, consider using the [SHUFFLE] hint on the **INSERT ... SELECT** statement. This hint makes the **INSERT** statement take longer, but reduces the number of output files generated. This technique can both avoid the "many small files" problem, and reduce the memory usage during the **INSERT** statement. (In the latest releases, Impala applies the [SHUFFLE] hint automatically if necessary, so this tip mainly applies to older Impala instances.)

```
INSERT INTO partitioned_parquet_table PARTITION (year, month, region)
   [SHUFFLE] SELECT c1, c2, c3, year, month, region FROM new_batch_of_raw_data;
```

Tutorial: Across the Fourth Dimension

One challenge in every programming language, operating system, or storage format is how to represent and manipulate date-based and time-based values. Let's look at how this works in Impala.

TIMESTAMP Data Type

In Impala, the one-stop shop for any temporal value is the TIMESTAMP data type. It can represent a date, a time, or both. It is stored in a consistent numeric format, relative to the Coordinated Universal Time (UTC) time zone to avoid issues with time zone translation. You can use TIMESTAMP as the data type for a table column, and pass or return values of that type using various built-in functions.

It has been traditional in Hadoop to represent date and time values as strings, and convert to a binary representation behind the scenes. Impala prefers to make TIMESTAMP a first-class data type; thus, some date- and time-related functions carried over from Hive have both STRING and TIMESTAMP variants in Impala.

Format Strings for Dates and Times

Impala recognizes strings with the format YYYY-MM-DD HH:MM:SS.sssssssss and can automatically convert those to TIMESTAMP values. A date or a time is allowed by itself, and the fractional second portion is optional for time values. To turn a string in some other format into a TIMESTAMP requires a two-step process: convert to an integer value with the unix_timestamp() function, which takes a string format argument; then convert that integer back into a TIMESTAMP.

The following example shows how a string 2014-12-01 in the standard notation can be directly converted to a TIMESTAMP, while the string 2014/12/01 requires converting to an integer and then back to a TIMESTAMP:

```
[localhost:21000] > select cast('2014-12-01' as timestamp);
+---------------------------------+
| cast('2014-12-01' as timestamp) |
+---------------------------------+
| 2014-12-01 00:00:00             |
+---------------------------------+
[localhost:21000] > select unix_timestamp('2014/12/01','yyyy/MM/dd');
+--------------------------------------+
| unix_timestamp('2014/12/01', 'yyyy/mm/dd') |
+--------------------------------------+
| 1417392000                           |
+--------------------------------------+
[localhost:21000] > select from_unixtime(
                  >    unix_timestamp('2014/12/01','yyyy/MM/dd')
                  > );
+---------------------------------------------------------+
| from_unixtime(unix_timestamp('2014/12/01', 'yyyy/mm/dd')) |
+---------------------------------------------------------+
| 2014-12-01 00:00:00                                     |
+---------------------------------------------------------+
[localhost:21000] > select from_unixtime(
                  >    unix_timestamp('12/01/2014','MM/dd/yyyy')
                  > );
+---------------------------------------------------------+
| from_unixtime(unix_timestamp('12/01/2014', 'mm/dd/yyyy')) |
+---------------------------------------------------------+
| 2014-12-01 00:00:00                                     |
+---------------------------------------------------------+
```

Working with Individual Date and Time Fields

Sometimes it's convenient to have access to the individual date and time fields. For example, if your table is partitioned by year and month, you can't just designate a TIMESTAMP value as the partition key, because then there would be a different partition for every hour, minute, second, and even microsecond. The table needs separate YEAR and MONTH columns, even if it also preserves the full date and time information as a TIMESTAMP column.

The way to get the separate fields is through the EXTRACT() function (new in Impala 1.4). It's important to keep these values as integer types—ideally, the smallest applicable ones such as TINYINT for anything up to 127, and SMALLINT for anything up to 32767— so they can be represented compactly in memory. That's another reason to avoid storing dates as strings, even though it might be convenient to represent months by their names, or days with leading zeros. It's easy to overlook this optimization tip, because you might not notice any storage savings on disk if you use text data files (where string and numeric values consume equal space) or partitioned tables (where the partition key columns are used as directory names, so string and numeric values are represented the same way). The storage and performance benefits become apparent when billions or trillions of these values are being compared, stored in hash tables in memory, or transmitted across the network between different machines in the cluster.

This example shows how you can pull out each individual field from a TIMESTAMP value. We make a tiny lookup table with the symbolic names of all of the fields for easy reference later:

```
CREATE TABLE UNITS (granularity TINYINT, unit STRING);
INSERT INTO units VALUES (1,'year'),(2,'month'),(3,'day'),(4,'hour'),
  (5,'minute'),(6,'second'),(7,'millisecond');

-- Get each date and time field from a single TIMESTAMP value.
SELECT unit, extract(now(), unit) FROM units ORDER BY granularity;
+-------------+----------------------+
| unit        | extract(now(), unit) |
+-------------+----------------------+
| year        | 2014                 |
| month       | 7                    |
| day         | 9                    |
| hour        | 13                   |
| minute      | 26                   |
| second      | 52                   |
| millisecond | 608                  |
+-------------+----------------------+
```

Date and Time Arithmetic

The TRUNC() function truncates a TIMESTAMP value down to the next lower year, week, day, quarter, and so on. This is a very useful technique for condensing a large number of date and time values down to a predictable number of combinations, either for doing GROUP BY queries or using the truncated values as partition key columns.

INTERVAL expressions let you add and subtract specific date and time increments to TIMESTAMP values. Any time you need to calculate a delta value (such as when an online auction ends), you can compute the appropriate TIMESTAMP by adding or subtracting some number of days, weeks, months, hours, and so on. You can chain a series of INTERVAL additions and subtractions to create a very precise delta value.

For example, you might strip off the time portion of a TIMESTAMP value so that you were left with just the date. Then you could add an INTERVAL expression to add back a specific time. Or you could use other kinds of INTERVAL addition or subtraction to create specific dates and times for reminders, deadlines, or other relative kinds of temporal values.

```
-- Get just the current date, no time.
[localhost:21000] > select trunc(now(), 'DD')
                  > as "first thing this morning";
```

```
+-------------------------+
| first thing this morning |
+-------------------------+
| 2014-07-09 00:00:00     |
+-------------------------+

[localhost:21000] > select trunc(now(), 'DD') + interval 8 hours
                  > as "8 AM this morning";
+---------------------+
| 8 am this morning   |
+---------------------+
| 2014-07-09 08:00:00 |
+---------------------+

[localhost:21000] > select now() + interval 2 weeks
                  > as "2 weeks from right now";
+------------------------------+
| 2 weeks from right now       |
+------------------------------+
| 2014-07-23 15:11:01.526788000 |
+------------------------------+

[localhost:21000] > select trunc(now(), 'DD') - interval 2 days + interval 15 hours
                  > as "3 PM, the day before yesterday";
+------------------------------+
| 3 pm, the day before yesterday |
+------------------------------+
| 2014-07-07 15:00:00          |
+------------------------------+
```

 Always double-check the unit argument when using the TRUNC()
function, because the argument values and some of their meanings
differ from the arguments to EXTRACT(). In particular, the 'DAY' argument to TRUNC() truncates to the first day of the week, while DD
truncates to the current day.

Let's Solve the Y2K Problem

Whenever I look at a new technology for storing and manipulating data, I ask myself
whether that technology makes it more or less likely to run into Y2K-style problems.
The Y2K problem arose because people designed data processing applications under
the assumption that year values could be stored as 2 digits, with an implicit base year
of 1900. This issue became critical in the year 2000, when the 2-digit years could no
longer be used for date arithmetic. I judge software systems based on how easy it is to
correct such problems if developers make assumptions that later turn out to be wrong.
This kind of flexibility is one of the key strengths of the Hadoop software stack.

The root of the Y2K problem was a desire to save money on expensive disk storage by saving two bytes per date field. Could such cost considerations still occur today? Hmm, if there are a billion rows, each extra byte represents another gigabyte of storage. Imagine a big web property with hundreds of millions of customers, and for each of those customers, you have to record a birthday, date joined, date of last visit, and so on. Two bytes per date field per customer adds up to a substantial number of gigabytes. Although everyone now knows not to leave the century out of year values, developers might still cut corners in their schema design for cost reasons, and those bad decisions might come back to bite them later.

As a thought experiment, let's construct a scenario with some Y2K-style bad data, and see how we could solve it in Impala.

 This is a simplified example, not a comprehensive treatment of the subject. Your mileage may vary. No warranty express or implied.

We start off with a data file constructed way back in the 20th century, with some names and birth dates in `MM-DD-YY` format, and whether the person is still living:

```
$ cat >20th_century.dat
John Smith,06-04-52,false
Jane Doe,03-22-76,true
^D
```

In the pre-Hadoop days, the original code parsed the birth date values as 2-digit or 2-character values, and filled in the 19 prefix whenever it needed to print any reports or do any arithmetic for the birth dates. Now, the company (which has a minimum age limit of 14) is just starting to sign up its first customers born in the 21st century. The new data file uses 4-digit years:

```
$ cat >2014_new_customers.dat
Adam Millennial,01-01-2000,true
Maria Sanchez,03-29-2001,true
^D
```

With Impala, there are several ways to solve this problem. Let's look at ways to make use of our SQL expertise (as opposed to just editing the original text data files):

```
CREATE TABLE inconsistent_data (name STRING, birthdate STRING, living BOOLEAN)
  ROW FORMAT DELIMITED FIELDS TERMINATED BY ",";
... Use 'hdfs dfs -put' command to move data files into appropriate Hadoop
... directories as demonstrated in earlier examples.

-- Make Impala aware of the newly added data files.
REFRESH inconsistent_data;
SELECT * FROM inconsistent_data;
```

```
+-----------------+------------+--------+
| name            | birthdate  | living |
+-----------------+------------+--------+
| Adam Millennial | 01-01-2000 | true   |
| Maria Sanchez   | 03-29-2001 | true   |
| John Smith      | 06-04-52   | false  |
| Jane Doe        | 03-22-76   | true   |
+-----------------+------------+--------+
```

At this point, we have a mixture of good and bad date values represented as strings. We'll construct some expressions to parse out the different month, day, and year portions. As we build a set of useful queries to transform the original values through a series of steps, we'll save each query as a view to keep each query readable and avoid a single monster query.

```
CREATE VIEW customer_data_separate_fields AS
  SELECT
  name,
  regexp_extract(birthdate,'([[:digit:]]+)-([[:digit:]]+)-([[:digit:]]+)', 1) month,
  regexp_extract(birthdate,'([[:digit:]]+)-([[:digit:]]+)-([[:digit:]]+)', 2) day,
  regexp_extract(birthdate,'([[:digit:]]+)-([[:digit:]]+)-([[:digit:]]+)', 3) year,
  living
  FROM inconsistent_data;
SELECT * FROM customer_data_separate_fields;
+-----------------+-------+-----+------+--------+
| name            | month | day | year | living |
+-----------------+-------+-----+------+--------+
| Adam Millennial | 01    | 01  | 2000 | true   |
| Maria Sanchez   | 03    | 29  | 2001 | true   |
| John Smith      | 06    | 04  | 52   | false  |
| Jane Doe        | 03    | 22  | 76   | true   |
+-----------------+-------+-----+------+--------+
```

The next step is to convert the separated-out fields to integer types instead of strings. Then we can do arithmetic on the dates.

```
CREATE VIEW customer_data_int_fields AS
  SELECT name, cast(month AS TINYINT) month,
    cast(day AS TINYINT) day,
    cast(year AS SMALLINT) year,
    living
    FROM customer_data_separate_fields;
```

Last, we identify the year values that were originally given as 2 digits, and convert those to 4-digit values from the 20th century. Any NULL values are passed through unchanged. Any year greater than 2 digits is passed through unchanged. (For simplicity, let's stipulate that this company does not have any customers born in the 1800s or earlier.)

```
CREATE VIEW customer_data_full_years AS
  SELECT name, month, day,
    CASE
      WHEN year IS NULL THEN NULL
```

```
        WHEN year < 100 THEN year + 1900
        ELSE year
    END
    AS year,
    living
FROM customer_data_int_fields;
```

Here we made a logical arrangement of the data that is more flexible and easier to extend and analyze. Even without changing the underlying data files, we accounted for 2-digit and 4-digit year values; we split up the original 3-part strings into separate fields; and we made the year, month, and day values into integers so that we could do arithmetic on them.

We can query the views to analyze the data in its cleaned up and reorganized form. Here we use a LIMIT clause to cap the number of rows returned, in case the back office loaded millions more rows in the meantime:

```
-- Doublecheck that the data is OK.
SELECT * FROM customer_data_full_years LIMIT 100;
+-----------------+-------+-----+------+--------+
| name            | month | day | year | living |
+-----------------+-------+-----+------+--------+
| John Smith      | 6     | 4   | 1952 | false  |
| Jane Doe        | 3     | 22  | 1976 | true   |
| Adam Millennial | 1     | 1   | 2000 | true   |
| Maria Sanchez   | 3     | 29  | 2001 | true   |
+-----------------+-------+-----+------+--------+
```

After running more queries to double-check that the data is entirely clean, we could make the new improved schema permanent and convert all the existing data files to a compact binary format. As we see in other examples using the Parquet format, the savings from this compression step are likely much greater than could be obtained by shortchanging the year values.

```
CREATE TABLE modernized_customer_data
    STORED AS PARQUET
    AS SELECT * FROM customer_data_full_years;
```

More Fun with Dates

The Impala TIMESTAMP data type has a range that starts on January 1, 1400 AD. Thus, for anything before that date, you would store separate integer fields for the year, month, day, and any time-related fields, rather than a single TIMESTAMP value that includes both date and time.

Applying the principle of using the smallest practical integer type, that means MONTH and DAY could always be TINYINT columns, and YEAR would depend on the time scale involved. Historians could use SMALLINT for their YEAR column to record years back to –32768 BC. Paleontologists could use INT to date fossils back to –2147483648 BC. And cosmologists could use BIGINT to chart time from the Big Bang to the future Big Crunch or heat death of the universe.

Pro Tip

The examples for schema evolution ("Tutorial: When Schemas Evolve" on page 89) show ways to deal with data where it is not immediately clear whether the existing values fit into the range for a particular integer type.

Tutorial: Verbose and Quiet impala-shell Output

In this book, I switch between verbose output in `impala-shell` when I need to show timing information for queries, or quiet mode for demonstrating features unrelated to performance. By default, an `impala-shell` session looks like this:

```
$ impala-shell -i localhost -d oreilly
...
[localhost:21000] > create table foo (x int);
Query: create table foo (x int); ❶
Returned 0 row(s) in 1.13s ❷
[localhost:21000] > select x from foo;
Query: select x from foo;
Returned 0 row(s) in 0.19s
```

❶ The way the statement is echoed back as a single line lets you copy and paste it, which is most useful for multiline statements that are hard to capture due to the continuation prompts.

❷ The time measurement is useful when you're comparing the performance of different query techniques and table structures, logging the output of a sequence of statements, or running the same statements multiple times to check if performance is consistent across runs.

A "quiet" session looks like this, without the query echoed back or the elapsed time for the query:

```
$ impala-shell -i localhost -d oreilly --quiet
[localhost:21000] > create table bar (s string);
[localhost:21000] > select s from bar;
```

This more compact form lets you see what's happening without all the extra informational messages.

The -B option produces an even more compact output style, with no ASCII boxes around the query results. You can think of -B as the "benchmark" option, because if all you want to do is get the results as fast as possible, suppressing the boxes lets impala-shell display the results much faster. The -B option is often used in combination with

`-q` (run a single query) or `-f` (run all the statements in a file), for benchmarking, setup scripts, or any kinds of automated jobs.

This example runs a single **SHOW TABLES** statement and then massages the results to produce a set of **DROP TABLE** statements, which are then stored in a *.sql* script file:

```
$ impala-shell -B --quiet -q 'show tables in oreilly' | \
  sed -e 's/^/drop table /' | sed -e 's/$/;/' | \
  tee drop_all_tables.sql
drop table bar;
drop table billion_numbers;
drop table billion_numbers_compacted;
...
```

This example runs a sequence of statements from an input file. Here we leave out the `--quiet` option because we are interested in the output showing the original query, and the time taken. We include the `-d` option to specify the database where all the queries should run, so that we do not need to use fully qualified table names.

```
$ impala-shell -d oreilly -B -f benchmark.sql
...some startup banner messages...
Query: use oreilly
Query: select count(*) from canada_facts
13
Returned 1 row(s) in 0.21s
Query: select count(*) from canada_regions
13
Returned 1 row(s) in 0.19s
Query: select count(*) from usa_cities
289
Returned 1 row(s) in 0.19s
```

Tutorial: When Schemas Evolve

One of the tenets of Hadoop is "schema on read," meaning that you're not required to do extensive planning up front about how your data is laid out, and you're not penalized if you later need to change or fine-tune your original decisions. Historically, this principle has clashed with the traditional SQL model where a **CREATE TABLE** statement defines a precise layout for a table, and data is reorganized to match this layout during the load phase. Impala bridges these philosophies in clever ways:

- Impala lets you define a schema for data files that you already have and immediately begin querying that data with no change to the underlying raw files.
- Impala does not require any length constraints for strings. No more trying to predict how much room to allow for the longest possible name, address, phone number, product ID, and so on.

- In the simplest kind of data file (using text format), fields can be flexibly interpreted as strings, numbers, timestamps, or other kinds of values.

- Impala allows data files to have more or fewer columns than the corresponding table. It ignores extra fields in the data file, and returns **NULL** if fields are missing from the data file. You can rewrite the table definition to have more or fewer columns and mix and match data files with the old and new column definitions.

- You can redefine a table to have more columns, fewer columns, or different data types at any time. The data files are not changed in any way.

- In a partitioned table, if newer data arrives in a different file format, you can change the definition of the table only for certain partitions, rather than going back and reformatting or converting all the old data.

- Impala can query data files stored outside its standard data repository. You could even point multiple tables (with different column definitions) at the same set of data files—for example, to treat a certain value as a string for some queries and a number for other queries.

The benefits of this approach include more flexibility, less time and effort spent converting data into a rigid format, and less resistance to the notion of fine-tuning the schema as needs change and you gain more experience. For example, if a counter exceeds the maximum value for an INT, you can promote it to a BIGINT with minimal hassle. If you originally stored postal codes or credit card numbers as integers and later received data values containing dashes or spaces, you could switch those columns to strings without reformatting the original data.

For example, the SAMPLE_DATA table used in several earlier examples has a column named ZEROFILL containing 6-digit integer values, including leading zeros where needed so that every value really has 6 characters. That field could be used to represent an encoded value where each digit or group of digits has some meaning, as with a credit card or telephone number. Treating that column as a STRING data type makes it easier to do SUBSTR() calls to pull out the first 3 digits, last 4 digits, or search and replace to get rid of optional punctuation characters, in the case of a phone number. Other times, it might be preferable to treat that column as a number, for example, to construct the next sequential value. Or what seems like a small range of values might later turn out to be a larger one, so you might initially treat it as a SMALLINT but then later change the column type to INT or BIGINT.

Regardless of how the column is defined, you can always use CAST() to convert its values to a different type during a query. What is the "best" type is a question of convenience, query readability, and efficiency. (Remember, your queries will likely process millions or billions of rows, so any unnecessary type conversions can add considerable overhead.) And when you convert to a binary file format such as Parquet or Avro, numbers can be stored more compactly than strings, potentially saving gigabytes of disk space for each byte you can remove from all the rows.

Impala lets you try out all these representations to see which one works best in practice. When the data is in a relatively unstructured file format, such as a delimited text file, you can make unlimited changes to the types and names of columns. Farther along the data pipeline, when the data files are in a structured format such as Parquet or Avro, the table schema is embedded in each data file and the changes you can make are more limited. For example, with Parquet you can change a column's type between TINYINT, SMALLINT, and INT, but not between other types such as STRING or TIMESTAMP.

You could also discover that some fields supplied in the data aren't really needed and so remove them from the table definition, or that new fields are useful and so add those to the table definition and any new data files. These techniques work in all file formats, but apply only to the last columns in the table, so define any optional or less-important columns last.

Numbers Versus Strings

In the following example, we first treat the ZEROFILL column as a string (its original definition) to find values starting with 0123:

```
SELECT zerofill FROM sample_data
  WHERE zerofill LIKE '0123%' LIMIT 5;
+----------+
| zerofill |
+----------+
| 012330   |
| 012372   |
| 012350   |
| 012301   |
| 012327   |
+----------+
Returned 5 row(s) in 0.57s
```

Next, we change the ZEROFILL column to a number, finding examples of even values, doing some arithmetic with the values, and ignoring the leading zeros:

```
ALTER TABLE sample_data
  CHANGE zerofill zerofill INT;
SELECT zerofill AS even, zerofill+1 AS odd
  FROM sample_data
  WHERE zerofill % 2 = 0 LIMIT 5;
+----------+--------+
| even     | odd    |
+----------+--------+
| 3838     | 3839   |
| 97464    | 97465  |
| 87046    | 87047  |
| 12158    | 12159  |
```

```
| 55478    | 55479  |
+----------+--------+
Returned 5 row(s) in 0.31s
```

Finally, we change ZEROFILL back to a string for some regular expression matching, to find values containing a sequence of three 1 digits.

 The CHANGE clause repeats the name ZEROFILL twice because it also sets a new name for the column; when changing only the data type, specify the same name again.

```
ALTER TABLE sample_data
  CHANGE zerofill zerofill STRING;
SELECT zerofill FROM sample_data
  WHERE zerofill REGEXP '1{3}' LIMIT 5;
+----------+
| zerofill |
+----------+
| 081116   |
| 031110   |
| 091118   |
| 011138   |
| 061110   |
+----------+
Returned 5 row(s) in 0.56s
```

Dealing with Out-of-Range Integers

If your table has values that are out of range for the specified integer type, they will be returned as the maximum value for the type. Thus, if you see numbers that bump up against the top of the range, you might need a bigger type for that column. Here is how you might deal with integer values where you do not know in advance whether their range will fit into the column type for an existing table.

Setup: Construct a table with some values that do not "fit" into the type of an integer column.

The column X starts off as a TINYINT, which can only hold a very limited range of values (–128 to 127).

```
CREATE TABLE unknown_range (x BIGINT);
INSERT INTO unknown_range VALUES (-50000), (-4000), (0), (75), (33000);
ALTER TABLE unknown_range CHANGE x x TINYINT;
```

Problem: We don't know if the –128 and 127 values are real, or signify out-of-range numbers.

We call the MIN_TINYINT() and MAX_TINYINT() functions, and later the equivalents for other types, so that we don't have to remember the exact ranges.

```
SELECT x FROM unknown_range LIMIT 10;
+------+
| x    |
+------+
| -128 |
| -128 |
| 0    |
| 75   |
| 127  |
+------+

SELECT count(x) AS "Suspicious values" FROM unknown_range
  WHERE x IN (min_tinyint(), max_tinyint());
+-------------------+
| suspicious values |
+-------------------+
| 3                 |
+-------------------+
```

Solution: Increase the size of the column and check against the allowed range, until there are no more suspicious values.

```
ALTER TABLE unknown_range CHANGE x x SMALLINT;
SELECT x FROM unknown_range LIMIT 10;
+--------+
| x      |
+--------+
| -32768 |
| -4000  |
| 0      |
| 75     |
| 32767  |
+--------+
SELECT count(x) AS "Suspicious values" FROM unknown_range
  WHERE x IN (min_smallint(), max_smallint());
+-------------------+
| suspicious values |
+-------------------+
| 2                 |
+-------------------+

ALTER TABLE unknown_range CHANGE x x INT;
SELECT x FROM unknown_range;
+--------+
| x      |
+--------+
| -50000 |
```

```
| -4000  |
| 0      |
| 75     |
| 33000  |
+--------+

SELECT count(x) AS "Suspicious values" FROM unknown_range
  WHERE x IN (min_smallint(), max_smallint());
+-------------------+
| suspicious values |
+-------------------+
| 0                 |
+-------------------+
```

At this point, you know the column is a large enough type to hold all the existing values without being larger than necessary and wasting space on disk and in memory.

Just as a refresher, here are the ranges for the different integer types:

```
[localhost:21000] > select min_bigint(), max_bigint();
+----------------------+---------------------+
| min_bigint()         | max_bigint()        |
+----------------------+---------------------+
| -9223372036854775808 | 9223372036854775807 |
+----------------------+---------------------+
[localhost:21000] > select min_int(), max_int();
+-------------+------------+
| min_int()   | max_int()  |
+-------------+------------+
| -2147483648 | 2147483647 |
+-------------+------------+
[localhost:21000] > select min_smallint(), max_smallint();
+----------------+----------------+
| min_smallint() | max_smallint() |
+----------------+----------------+
| -32768         | 32767          |
+----------------+----------------+
[localhost:21000] > select min_tinyint(), max_tinyint();
+---------------+---------------+
| min_tinyint() | max_tinyint() |
+---------------+---------------+
| -128          | 127           |
+---------------+---------------+
```

If you need a larger integer than MAX_BIGINT(), you can define a DECIMAL(*n*). The maximum value for *n* is 38, which can hold up to 999999... (9 repeated 38 times).

Tutorial: Levels of Abstraction

SQL shares some of the convenience of functional programming languages, where the end result is built from multiple layers, each performing some easily understood transformation. Whatever result you get from a query, you can enhance the results further by running individual columns through an additional function, or layering another query on top by using a WITH clause or a subquery, or pushing down the complexity by turning the query into a view.

String Formatting

In this example, we received some string data that is not in the optimal format. It is in all lowercase, and it has double quotes around the values, which is not appropriate for Impala text data. We run the string columns through a regular expression function to remove leading and trailing quotation marks. Then we run the result through another formatting function to capitalize the first letter. After finding the right combination of functions to achieve the desired output, we embed the details in a view, which hides the complexity of the function calls and makes subsequent queries more readable.

```
SELECT * FROM bad_format;
+------------+-----------+
| first_name | last_name |
+------------+-----------+
| "john"     | "smith"   |
| "jane"     | "doe"     |
+------------+-----------+

SELECT regexp_replace(first_name,'(^"|"$)','') AS first_name
  FROM bad_format;
+------------+
| first_name |
+------------+
| john       |
| jane       |
+------------+

SELECT initcap(regexp_replace(first_name,'(^"|"$)','')) AS first_name
  FROM bad_format;
+------------+
| first_name |
+------------+
| John       |
| Jane       |
+------------+

CREATE VIEW good_format AS
  SELECT initcap(regexp_replace(first_name,'(^"|"$)','')) AS first_name,
    initcap(regexp_replace(last_name,'(^"|"$)','')) AS last_name
  FROM bad_format;
```

```
SELECT * FROM good_format;
+-------------+-----------+
| first_name  | last_name |
+-------------+-----------+
| John        | Smith     |
| Jane        | Doe       |
+-------------+-----------+
```

Temperature Conversion

This example uses a subquery in the `WITH` clause to evaluate a temperature conversion formula and then runs calculations on the converted values. This is a handy technique to avoid repeating complicated expressions multiple times. Because the `WITH` clause does not create any permanent object, you avoid cluttering the namespace with new tables or views.

```
WITH celsius_temps AS
  (SELECT (degrees_f - 32) * 5 / 9 AS degrees_c FROM fahrenheit_temps)
SELECT min(degrees_c), max(degrees_c), avg(degrees_c) FROM celsius_temps;
```

This example encodes the Fahrenheit-to-Celsius conversion formula in a view, then filters the converted data by querying the view, referring only to the Celsius values.

```
CREATE VIEW celsius_temps AS SELECT (degrees_f - 32) * 5 / 9 AS degrees_c,
  year, month, day, location FROM fahrenheit_temps;
SELECT max(degrees_c), min(degrees_c) FROM celsius_temps
  WHERE year = 1999 AND degrees_c BETWEEN -40 and 40;
```

This example builds another view on top of the first one, to take a numeric value and do some string formatting to make it suitable for use in a report. The final query doesn't need to know anything about the original Fahrenheit values or the raw numbers used in the report.

```
CREATE VIEW celsius_pretty_printed AS
  SELECT concat(cast(degrees_c as string)," degrees Celsius") AS degrees_c,
  year, month, day, location FROM celsius_temps;
SELECT degrees_c, year, month, day location FROM celsius_pretty_printed
  WHERE year = 1998 ORDER BY year, month, day;
```

About the Author

John Russell is a software developer and technical writer, and he's currently the documentation lead for the Cloudera Impala project. He has a broad range of database and SQL experience from previous roles on industry-leading teams. For DB2, he designed and coded the very first Information Center. For Oracle Database, he documented application development subjects and designed and coded the Project Tahiti doc search engine. For MySQL, he documented the InnoDB storage engine. Originally from Newfoundland, Canada, John now resides in Berkeley, California.

Colophon

The animal on the cover of *Getting Started with Impala* is an impala (*Aepyceros melampus*). This is a medium-sized antelope native to the continent of Africa, which lives in savanna and brushland habitats. They are herbivores, and spend their days in herds grazing on grass and other vegetation.

Male impalas are the only sex with horns, which curve in an S shape rather like the lyre (an instrument of ancient Greece). These horns are used to fight other males during breeding season and to protect territory. Males are also noticeably larger and heavier than females: 30–36 inches tall at the shoulder and 120–160 pounds, versus the females' average of 28–33 inches and 90–120 pounds. All impalas have brown coats, black stripes on their rear legs, and a white tail with a black stripe running down its length.

Impalas live in three kinds of social groups during the rainy season when mating occurs: bachelor herds of nonterritorial and young males, herds of territorial males with breeding females, and herds of females with their young. Young male impalas remain in the latter kind of group until they are about four years old, when they reach sexual maturity and establish their own territory. In the dry season, these groups often intermingle.

Impalas are very fast runners, which is their main defense against natural predators such as lions, cheetahs, crocodiles, and hyenas. They can also leap nearly 10 feet in the air, which serves as a tactic to confuse or startle predators.

Many of the animals on O'Reilly covers are endangered; all of them are important to the world. To learn more about how you can help, go to *animals.oreilly.com*.

The cover image is from Wood's *Animate Creation*. The cover fonts are URW Typewriter and Guardian Sans. The text font is Adobe Minion Pro; the heading font is Adobe Myriad Condensed; and the code font is Dalton Maag's Ubuntu Mono.

Have it your way.

Get even more for your money.

Join the O'Reilly Community, and register the O'Reilly books you own. It's free, and you'll get:

- $4.99 ebook upgrade offer
- 40% upgrade offer on O'Reilly print books
- Membership discounts on books and events
- Free lifetime updates to ebooks and videos
- Multiple ebook formats, DRM FREE
- Participation in the O'Reilly community
- Newsletters
- Account management
- 100% Satisfaction Guarantee

Signing up is easy:

1. Go to: oreilly.com/go/register
2. Create an O'Reilly login.
3. Provide your address.
4. Register your books.

Note: English-language books only

To order books online:
oreilly.com/store

For questions about products or an order:
orders@oreilly.com

To sign up to get topic-specific email announcements and/or news about upcoming books, conferences, special offers, and new technologies:
elists@oreilly.com

For technical questions about book content:
booktech@oreilly.com

To submit new book proposals to our editors:
proposals@oreilly.com

O'Reilly books are available in multiple DRM-free ebook formats. For more information:
oreilly.com/ebooks

CPSIA information can be obtained at www.ICGtesting.com
Printed in the USA
BVOW08s2019300914

368982BV00006B/12/P